Rosalynn Carter

Her Life Story

Other Books by

DAWN LANGLEY SIMMONS

  Biography
Vinnie Ream: the Girl Who Sculptured Lincoln
A Rose for Mrs. Lincoln
Osceola
The Two Lives of Baby Doe
Princess Margaret
The Sawdust Trail (A History of American Evangelism)
Lady Bird and Her Daughters
Jacqueline Kennedy (with Ann Pinchot)
Golden Boats From Burma

  Autobiography
All For Love

  Biographical Novel
The Gypsy Condesa

Rosalynn with her mother, Allie Murray Smith, as she received
the Georgia College (Milledgeville, Ga.) Alumni Mother of the
Year Award. *Wide World Photos*

Rosalynn Carter

Her Life Story

Dawn Langley Simmons

Illustrated

Fell's Books Fill Your Needs

FREDERICK FELL PUBLISHERS, INC.
NEW YORK

ISBN 0-8119-0301-X

For information address:

Frederick Fell Publishers, Inc.
386 Park Avenue South
New York, New York 10016

Published simultaneously in Canada by:
Thomas Nelson & Sons, Limited
Don Mills, Ontario, Canada

MANUFACTURED IN THE UNITED STATES OF AMERICA

1 2 3 4 5 6 7 8 9 0

Designed by Michael U. Polvere

For
My Daughter
Natasha

To have roots is so important. Everybody needs a place they call home, a place that doesn't change. When I go home to Plains, I know people there care for me. I think that's one thing about Jimmy that appealed to people—he did have roots, he did have that stability, a sense of belonging and knowing who you are.

Rosalynn Carter

Acknowledgments

THREE years ago when a national weekly first sent me on assignment, with my then four-year-old daughter, Natasha Manigault Paul, to write articles on Plains, Georgia, and its most illustrious family, the Carters, I must confess I was less than enthusiastic. Two weeks later I returned completely intrigued by the family that then hoped to see its eldest son become President of the United States.

Staying in local homes with neighbors who had known the Carters all their lives, I listened to dozens of stories and anecdotes concerning "Mr. Jimmy" and his Rosalynn.

Miss Lillian was most gracious and a note made in my diary at the time says simply: "She reminds me of Mother Rutherford. She has the same wrinkles that are delightful when she laughs. She likes children and gave Natasha a picture of her son signed:

FOR NATASHA FROM JIMMY'S MAMA "

"Mr. Alton"—Alton Carter, known as "Uncle Buddy" in the family—was especially generous with his time on several subsequent visits and, at the suggestion of the

xi

0268360

112370

White House, briefed me on the Carter's family history. I grieved when Mr. Alton died, for in spite of his great age he was one of those ever young people. He had a certain quality that made him stand out in a crowd. My daughter will always remember "Mr. Alton" for he gave her a milk glass dish with the Lord's Prayer written upon it, a fitting gift from the venerable uncle of the man who would soon be President of the United States.

Mr. Alton was especially proud of Rosalynn Carter, his niece by marriage, and the way she had taken her solo campaign for her husband's election out on the road.

"She is a sweet, simple girl," he told me. "She never was and still isn't a blabbermouth . . . And coming from dear, blunt "Uncle Buddy" that was praise indeed.

The women of Plains, in whose homes I drank coffee, were loud in their praises of the woman who would be First Lady. As Ida English (Miss Ida), an excellent soup maker, said emphatically, "Next to her mother, Miss Allie, Rosalynn is the best woman with a needle in Plains."

I would like to thank the following for their courtesy in helping me with the writing of this book: Miss Lillian for being so outspokenly honest and so kind to a small girl on a very hot day, and Miss Amy Carter who gave Natasha some colored pictures to amuse her; Miss Allie, Rosalynn's mama, who I found shared my love for burning trash; the late Alton Carter; Mr. and Mrs. W. C. English (Miss Ida); Mr. Billy Carter; the Reverend and Mrs. Bruce Edwards (Mr. Edwards is the former pastor of Plains Baptist Church); Mr. and Mrs. Howard Colston (Miss Sara); their daughter and grandson, Tim Speck, for generous hospitality; Deacon and Mrs. Ernest Turner (Miss June); Jo-Ann Gordy Vincent; Richard Little, Director, Public Relations, Georgia Southwestern College, Americus, Georgia, and his Staff for their many kindnesses in checking research; the British Information Services, New York City; Patricia Hollowbread of Hornchurch, Essex, England,for European research; Susan Marcell, Reference Resources Librarian, University of Virginia Library, Charlotteville, Virginia; Dena Crane, Director of the Greene County, New York, Council For the Arts; Raymond Bissett, Designer, and West Grant, Atlanta, Georgia; Mrs. Pat Hollander, Chief Librarian, and the Staff of Catskill Public Library, New York; Dorothy Augustine, formerly Chief Librarian of the same library; Liz Smith, Columnist of the *New York Daily News* for help and inspiration; Sybil Tannenbaum, Laura Romak; Jean da Luca; Jim Henry Motsinger of Lewisburg, Kentucky; the Research Department, *Atlanta Journal-Constitution.*; Barbara Holdridge; Florence Haskell; Mary Kaye Hardee; Rosabelle Waites; Olga and Salvatore Verde; Evelyn Bernell; Ritchia Barloga Atkinson; my sister, Mrs. James Larkin (Fay Doreen) of Sissinghurst, Kent, England; Edwin Peacock of Charleston, South Carolina, Hyman J. Fechter, Attorney-at-Law; Virginia Calvo, Barbara Newcombe, Fay Levinn, Jean Meadow, Nita Blauberg, Ann Lasher, Stephanie Gaffney, and Rai Schmalz, all of the Greene County Travel Agency, Catskill, New York; and last but not least, my publisher Fred Fell, who gave me encouragement in snowy Catskill from his sunny winter home in Florida; and his ever patient and encouraging editor, Gail North.

Resurgum House,
Catskill, N.Y.

Rosalynn, daughter Amy, and sister-in-law Ruth Carter Stapleton walk across the street to Blair House to visit the wife of Spanish Prime Minister Adolfo Suarez. *Wide World Photos*

Prologue

FIRST Lady Rosalynn Carter was resting in her bedroom at the White House. It had been a long, busy day and she was nearly asleep. Suddenly she became aware of comings and goings in the family quarters. Then Amy came in, her blue eyes bright with excitement.

"Who's there?" Rosalynn asked.

"It's the king," announced Amy in that special way children have of letting their mothers into a big secret.

The President had brought his royal visitor, then a lonely widower recovering from the untimely death of his beloved queen, to visit his nine-year-old daughter.

Amy, who was propped up in her four-poster bed reading a book, had taken it all in stride. She had been meeting visiting dignitaries since she was a three-year-old living in the Georgia Governor's Mansion.

*   *   *

President Jimmy Carter is a family man blessed with a wife who, in months of campaigning alone across the United States, helped more than anyone else in electing him to office.

15

He calls her, "My sweetheart . . . the only woman I have ever loved," and bridles when critics dub her the "Steel Magnolia."

Theirs has been a union blessed with domestic felicity, loving and working as they have in extraordinary harmony. Not since the young Kennedys, with their brief, bright dream of Camelot, have so attractive a President and his First Lady set out to revitalize the spirit of the nation.

When Rosalynn Carter said she would attempt to better the lot of the elderly, it was no idle talk. She had watched her mother, Allie Smith, cry for a week when she was forced by her age to retire from her job with the post office in Plains. Advancing years did not make a person superfluous. Jimmy's mother, Miss Lillian, had joined the Peace Corps at sixty-eight, setting out to nurse lepers in India.

The President once said, "If Mother Allie hadn't brought up Rosalynn the way she did, I would probably not be President." Widowed at thirty-four, with four children to support, of which 13-year-old Rosalynn, was the eldest, Miss Allie supported her family by working as a seamstress. Rosalynn helped all she could, caring for the younger children and working after school as a shampooer in a beauty shop. From her mother she learned self-discipline, one of her most admirable traits as First Lady.

When well-meaning people talk of her underprivileged childhood, Rosalynn is quick to reassure them:

"I never felt poor. We never went hungry; we had a cow and a garden. We had our own home. My mother, who is a wonderful seamstress, made my clothes, and everyone always admired them. So although we didn't have a lot of money, I was never concerned about it."

Gloria Carter Spann, Jimmy's sister, recalls Rosalynn's clothes. "Her mother made them. I still remember her circular skirt with tulips appliqued around the border."

"I take after my Mother, who looks much younger than she is," says the First Lady, "because she worked all her life, was active, and didn't depend on anyone."

*   *   *

Rosalynn Carter is very much her own woman, and the President is the first to admit it. "I've never won an argument with her," he has jokingly said. "And the only times I thought I had, I found out the argument wasn't over yet."

In the beginning, young and immature as they were (she was only eighteen when they married), they had problems adjusting to one another. Once they had grown to understand one another better, they found what he calls their "precious relationship." Neither attempts to dominate the other.

He watched with pride when, in June 1977, she set off for a solo, seven-nation tour of Latin America. Not since the days of Eleanor Roosevelt had a First Lady attempted such a venture. Rosalynn's knowledge and understanding of the problems of the countries she visited deeply impressed her Latin American hosts. In 1978 she captured the hearts of West Germans when, quite spontaneously, she danced a polka in the streets with the burgomaster of Linz.

Yet it is in the field of mental health that First Lady Rosalynn Carter wants most to be remembered by history. Already she is said to have persuaded the President to authorize $300 million to be used for community mental health programs.

Behind every great man there is an equally great woman. Franklin Roosevelt had Eleanor, Winston Churchill his Clementine . . . and *Jimmy Carter his Rosalynn.*

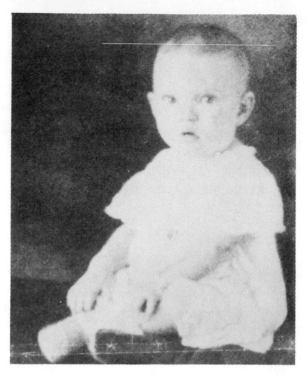

Rosalynn's first baby picture.

Rosalynn at five.

_1_

"SHE was a good baby and a good girl," says Allie Smith, Rosalynn Carter's mother.

Rosalynn (pronounced *Rose-a-lun* according to Miss Allie, as the First Lady's mother is always called in Plains) was born on the family farm five miles south of town, August 18, 1927, at six o'clock in the morning. Her mother's family, the Murrays, were of Irish-Scotch stock and had once lived on the fabled Isle of Skye.

Rosalynn's father, Wilburn Edgar Smith, could boast direct descent from Captain John Smith's cousin. The captain, associated in American folk lore with the Indian princess Pocohontas, persuaded Edgar Smith's forebear to make the long and dangerous voyage to America. From such romantic beginnings, history and a future First Lady were made.

A pretty child with a touch of that stubbornness characteristic of her father's family, Rosalynn was the eldest of four children. Jerrold (Jerry), Murray, and Allethea came later.

Miss Allie was a good but firm mother, who believed first in her children being obedient. Of Rosalynn she says, "Usually she obeyed us, but when she didn't, she would be spanked. I remember the time when she ran across the street to play with a neighbor without telling me. I worried because she crossed the street alone. When I punished her with a switching, she got angry, but she didn't do it again."

As Rosalynn grew older and the other children came along she became a real little mother to all of them. They called her "Sister" and still do as adults.

As the eldest girl, Rosalynn was close to her father, who is remembered in Plains as "a very good mechanic." He also drove the school bus. When Edgar became desperately sick with leukemia, Rosalynn took it hard.

Living over in Archery, a dot on the map near Plains, was Lillian Gordy Carter, the wife of a wealthy farmer, a registered nurse, and, according to the neighbors, something of an eccentric. Mrs. Carter went out and gave her professional services to the poor regardless of race—"the underdogs of Georgia" as she called them. Among her patients was Rosalynn's father, whom Miss Lillian had known since he was a boy. Edgar was a friend of Earl Carter, her husband, who turned a blind eye to his wife's ministering to blacks as well as whites.

"He was a very good man," Miss Lillian says of Edgar Smith. "It was a rare privilege to care for him."

Every evening she visited the Smith home for three hours to give the dying Edgar his injections and treatment as prescribed by the doctor. It also gave the devoted Miss Allie and 13-year-old Rosalynn a rest.

During these visits, Miss Lillian liked to talk of her own children, especially her eldest boy, Jimmy, a studious youngster who was then a high school senior. The Smiths found these stories a welcome relief to the sadness that had invaded their home. They liked the story of the billy goat best:

1945 GALE Yearbook photo of Rosalynn Smith.
Courtesy: Georgia Southwestern College

When Jimmy was two years old, he was stricken with a serious attack of colitis. He was in critical condition when he was admitted to the local Wise Sanitarium, where he had been born. All he kept asking for was a billy goat. Undaunted by this unusual request, Gussie Abrams Howell, the hospital's Director of Nursing, found Jimmy what he wanted. She tied the billy goat to the little boy's bed, so he could talk to him and pet him . . . And, of course, with such sympathetic treatment, Jimmy soon recovered.

Other stories about Jimmy's adventures with animals also entertained the Smiths. When Jimmy was ten, he went on a fishing trip to Florida and returned with a baby alligator, which, to his sisters' dismay, he kept in a cardboard box under his bed. On another occasion Jimmy found the babies of a squirrel that had just been killed by hunters. He named the two orphans "Pete" and "Repete" and began raising them with an eyedropper. For a time they rode everywhere on his shoulders.

The Smiths must also have been touched by the early signs of Jimmy's understanding and compassion that turned up in another of Miss Lillian's stories. Once, as a little boy, Jimmy began crying when he saw his father shooting sparrows. He had remembered the Sunday school story that not a single sparrow fell to the ground that the Lord didn't know about. When Earl Carter saw how upset his son was, he immediately stopped the shooting.

Rosalynn, of course, listened enthralled to all the stories. Jimmy was the best looking boy at school, and all the girls had crushes on him, including her.

*　　*　　*

After several months of suffering, Edgar Smith died leaving his widow and young family nearly penniless. Miss

Allie rented the farm and proceeded to support her family by doing something she had always enjoyed—sewing. She made everything from wedding gowns to gentlemen's winter overcoats. In those days the most she ever got for an overcoat was five dollars. Often, when Miss Allie had to meet a deadline with an order, Rosalynn helped with the sewing. In time she became almost as clever with a needle as her mother. Years later when she went to live in the White House, the only item of furniture Rosalynn brought along was her previous sewing machine.

A year after Edgar's untimely death, Allie's own mother died, leaving her with nobody to lean on for advice. Rosalynn never forgot those frugal days or the way her beloved mother grew to be an independent woman: "I saw her develop into a very strong person who took over the family. She had never even supported herself, but she sent us all through school. She sewed for other people; when she became postmistress in Plains. I was the oldest, and that tends to make you more responsible, but there was so much more I could have done."

*   *   *

Rosalynn's lifelong habit of working hardest at whatever was most difficult for her began during her schooldays. "She was an excellent student," her mother proudly remembers, and like Jimmy and all the Carters, she was an avid reader. Rarely did she have to ask for help with her homework. Social studies were her most difficult subject, and she would tell Miss Allie to wake her at five in the morning so that she could go over these lessons several times before the school bus came.

At Plains High School, Rosalynn played with the basketball team, and in a contest based on beauty and brains, she was voted "May Queen of Plains." People also admired the blue-eyed girl with the curly brown hair for the selfless way she helped care for her younger brothers and sister. After school she worked in a local beauty shop, for the family needed every cent it could earn. By the time she left high school she had learned the value of a dollar, something she can never forget.

"She's real saving at times," Miss Allie says with a smile.

In those days Rosalynn was noticeably shy and retiring with only one close girl friend, Jimmy's sister, who was destined to become America's most famous woman evangelist, Ruth Carter Stapleton. Rosalynn often visited the Carter family home to see Ruth. "Precious, darling, and so beautiful," is how Miss Lillian remembers Rosalynn then. "Rosalynn was Ruth's best friend. Every weekend she was at our house when Ruth wasn't at her home in Plains."

Ruth remembers the concern for others that so often guided the actions of her best teenage friend: "Rosalynn had naturally curly hair. She could wash it and just comb it, and it curled. Mine always had to be rolled up or it looked stringy. So she would try to fix my hair until it looked as nice as hers. And when her mother would make Rosalynn a dress, she would ask her to make me one just like it, only in a different color."

By this time Jimmy was away studying at the Naval Academy in Annapolis. Rosalynn was three years younger than Jimmy, and if he noticed her at all, it was just as a friend of his sister Ruth. As for Rosalynn, she thought that Jimmy Carter was just about the most handsome man she had ever seen.

"He was older and so good looking" are her own glowing words.

"I guess I always idolized him."

*   *   *

As a student at Plains High School, Rosalynn's life, like Jimmy's, was enriched by Julia Lewis Coleman. "Miss Julia" to her students, she was nicknamed "Sweet" by her fellow teachers. The daughter of a minister, she was born in Mississippi in 1889, moving to Plains as a child. She graduated from the local high school before going on to Bessie Tift College in Forsyth, Georgia, a much respected Baptist institution. She graduated with the class of 1908.

From that day on her vocation became the education of the youth of Plains. She often said that she never found the time to get married.

Although her one leg was shorter than the other as a result of a childhood fall and eye bleedings while in college left her with poor sight, Miss Julia was always noted for her cheerful disposition. Accomplished as poet and pianist, she made it her business to meet artists and writers during the school vacations.

The knowledge gleaned from the trips she took during her vacations she brought back to her students. Of Miss Julia, Jimmy Carter, her most famous student, proudly says, "She required us to look at pictures and paintings, to listen to opera. She brought enrichment into our lives."

*   *   *

Rosalynn graduated from high school in 1944. There were only eleven other students in her class, and she was the valedictorian. She then matriculated at Georgia Southwestern College in nearby Americus, and two years later she chose interior decorating as her major. With a budget of four dollars a week, Rosalynn sometimes went without lunch in order to see a movie. She was active in the college tumbling club and its Young Democrats, the latter a taste of things to come.

When Jimmy Carter came home for the holidays, she tried harder than ever to get him to notice her. Of course, they had known each other all their lives, but during high school when she was 13, he was already a senior and, as she recalls, "just about the best student in school." If he hadn't slipped off to Americus with some other boys the last day of his final year, he would have been the valedictorian.

However, five years later Rosalynn Smith had blossomed into a very lovely young woman with a fragile Staffordshire-shepherdess-like beauty. She was very shy compared to his witty, outspoken mother. Jimmy was a midshipman; the chemistry was right.

She had often heard the story from Miss Lillian and Ruth of how much Jimmy had wanted to attend the Naval Academy. Miss Lillian, as usual, told it best:

"He was too short, too thin and had flat feet . . . So, he exercised, he ate bananas, and he rolled a Coke bottle under his arch for hours."

Ruth had told Rosalynn how proud both her parents were when Jimmy was finally accepted for Annapolis, but when it came time for them to part with their eldest son, the grief they felt was almost too much to bear. After the good-byes were over, Earl Carter walked off in one direction, and Miss Lillian went to the Pond House, got into a boat, and went fishing. Both parents had to be alone with their memories.

*   *   *

Rosalynn recalls the midshipman days: "I really fell all over myself just to get Jimmy to notice me. I'd dress up and go over to the Carters' to see Ruth, and I'd act as adult as I could, but Jimmy wouldn't pay me any attention."

Rosalynn Smith, Vice President
of the Sophomore Class. Georgia
Southwestern College, 1946.

Courtesy: Georgia
Southwestern College

1946 photograph of teenage
Rosalynn Smith, taken from the
GALE, publication of Georgia
Southwestern College.

Finally, one night Jimmy and some other fellows were arranging their own private dance complete with jukebox music at the Pond House. He invited Ruth and Rosalynn by, tactfully suggesting they get somebody else to bring them. During the evening Jimmy danced once with his sister and then with Rosalynn to whom he made the ungallant remark, "Don't you think the girl I brought is pretty?"

Rosalynn saw red. "She's not half as pretty as I am."

According to Miss Lillian, "At that moment, Jimmy noticed Rosalynn for the first time." Shortly afterwards he took Rosalynn Smith to the movies at Americus in a rumble-seated Ford on a double date with Ruth and her boyfriend. He never dated another girl.

Later in the Carter family kitchen where he still read books while he ate, Jimmy told his mother, "She's the girl I want to marry."

He proposed that Christmas, and Rosalynn's answer was no.

By George Washington's Birthday, when, at Jimmy's invitation, Rosalynn attended the Naval Academy's famed Ring Dance, she had changed her mind and said yes.

Then Jimmy Carter sent Miss Allie, his future mother-in-law whom he has ever after affectionately called "Mother Allie," a touching letter asking for her daughter's hand in marriage. "He wrote that he loved her, promised to take good care of her, and told me not to worry, that her life would be happy," said Miss Allie, as in 1978 she greeted visitors to Plains, surrounded by bowls of blossoming wild yellow cacti.

Rosalynn was only 18 and Jimmy three years older when they were married July 7, 1946, in Plains Methodist Church, where the Smiths were members.

The young bride, who did not want a big wedding, arrived late for the ceremony with her bridegroom. This was unusual for Jimmy Carter, always the most punctual of men. The organist was already on the second round of the "Wedding March" when the couple dashed hand in hand up the aisle.

Jimmy wore his navy dress whites while his bride's afternoon dress was offset with a halo-type hat made popular by that most famous of American brides, Wallis Warfield Simpson, when she married Britain's former King Edward VIII. Following the ceremony, the happy Ensign and Mrs. Jimmy Carter left for a honeymoon in Chimney Rock, North Carolina.

From that day forward they have lived only for each other.

_2_

A FTER the honeymoon Rosalynn lived on the naval base at Norfolk, Virginia, while Jimmy was assigned to a battleship in the harbor. She was not so homesick as her family predicted she would be. Jimmy was now her whole life, and she was blissfully happy.

Most young girls of her generation stayed in Plains after their graduations, married local boys, and raised new families there. Rosalynn was the exception, and she did not regret it one bit. Up until her marriage, that one visit to the Naval Academy at Annapolis with all its rich historical traditions had been the greatest adventure of her life. That she had failed to mail her application to Georgia State College, where she had planned to earn a bachelor's degree, and had married Jimmy instead did not worry her at all. She was Mrs. Jimmy Carter, and at that point in her life, he was all she wanted.

Wistfully recalling those first happy days as newly weds, Jimmy has said, "I was by far the dominant person in the marriage at the beginning."

Even then Rosalynn was a woman apart from the other young wives on the base. She abhorred coffee klatches and the little gossipy get-togethers so enjoyed by her neighbors. When Jimmy came home he brought her new books to read, including one on great masterpieces of art. They both vividly remembered their school days with Miss Julia Coleman when she had introduced them both in turn to the fascinating world of painting and sculpture. Now, as young-marrieds, they continued their art studies together.

"We just enjoyed it," says Rosalynn. From these modest beginnings Jimmy and Rosalynn Carter acquired a warm appreciation for a subject they both loved. In addition, they absorbed a great deal of information concerning their own country's creative achievements. Concerning the outcome of those early art studies in Norfolk, Roy Slade, former director of the Corcoran Gallery of Art, Washington, and currently President of the Cranbrook Academy of Art, Bloomfield Hills, Michigan, says, "I was absolutely overwhelmed by Jimmy's knowledge of American art."

When Rosalynn learned she was pregnant, she and Jimmy held hands and prayed together. They hoped that this first child would be a boy. When he asked if she would like to go home to Plains for the birth, she absolutely refused to leave him. Plains and the hardships she had endured for the last few years since her father's premature death were behind her forever, or so she thought. The streak of independence she had inherited from the Scottish Murrays was evident now. Together the young Jimmy Carters waited for the baby to arrive, and when he did on July 3, 1947, they named him John William after Rosalynn's grandfather. They were soon calling him "Jackie."

He was a beautiful baby, fat, chubby, and surprisingly good. Rosalynn had had plenty of practice in child raising from her younger brothers and sister. She was a devoted mother; Jackie was always immaculate. Even then Rosa-

does now, that a job worth doing is worth doing well. Nothing was ever out of place in the small apartment. When Jimmy came off the ship, he never once had cause to complain. The wife he had chosen back home in Plains had proved her worth in Norfolk.

"I had to take care of everything," Rosalynn remembers. "I was completely on my own, without friends or family, because Jimmy went to sea so often. At first I didn't think I could raise our children by myself, but I did what I had to do."

She was also painfully shy in those days. Some of the other young officer's wives thought Rosalynn Carter standoffish. She wasn't really. Mrs. Carter's life now revolved exclusively around Jimmy and the new baby. She did not particularly want to discuss or share them with anybody.

Three years later a second son, James Earl III—but always to be known as "Chip" in the family—was born in Hawaii on April 12, 1950. Rosalynn and Jackie had followed Jimmy to his first base in San Diego, Caifornia, and then to Oahu, Hawaii. Because she had never before left the continental United States, moving to the fabled islands was like a fairy tale to the girl from rural Georgia.

Jimmy and Rosalynn decided to make the best of the opportunity given them to study another culture and, in spite of the two babies, extended their interests to include Hawaiian history. Rosalynn even found time to take hula lessons, and, like everything else she has determined to master in her life, she excelled at it. She never did hula in public, however. Only Jimmy and members of the family have been privileged to see her perform.

Jimmy and Rosalynn could soon pride themselves on their knowledge of Hawaiian history. They became interested in the stories of the great kings and queens of the lush green islands, particularly the legendary Kamehameha I (1736–1819) who united the island kingdoms in

33

1810. His son, Kamehameha II, and his queen were other favorites. They had taken an ill-fated trip to England, where they both died rather ignobly of the measles.

Rosalynn would take Jackie to see the gleaming bronze statue of Kamehameha I in his golden robes that stands in front of the judiciary building. They also liked watching the colors being raised and lowered each morning and evening by a naval honor guard over the partially sunken wreck of the battleship *Arizona*, which was lost in the Japanese attack on Pearl Harbor, December 7, 1941.

Two years later the Carters moved again, this time to New London, Connecticut, where Rosalynn entered a local hospital for the birth of their third child. Both she and Jimmy had prayed hard for a girl, but it was not to be. Jeffrey, quickly shortened to "Jeff," was born April 18, 1952. If they were disappointed at not getting their much longed for daughter, it was not for long. Jeff was a lively baby who learned to smile at a few weeks. As he grew older he joined his two brothers in exercising that family prerogative, the Jimmy Carter toothy grin.

*   *   *

As practically a single parent, Rosalynn's time was fully occupied with her children. Her mother and the rest of the family wrote often. Miss Allie was doing well at the post office, where she had really found a job worthy of her good-natured talents. To Rosalynn, Plains seemed far away; travel and motherhood had matured her mind. The wonderful stories that Jimmy brought back for those longed for reunions from duty at sea more than replaced the gossip from home.

Through it all, the young Carters were still deeply religious. She was not surprised when he told her of the Easter services he had conducted in a submarine torpedo room.

34

"Religion," he impressed on Rosalynn, "is like breathing." He was only 11 years old when, after attending several revival meetings, he had offered himself for baptism in the tank by the pulpit of Plains First Baptist Church. At Annapolis he had often been teased by fellow cadets for being a Georgia farm boy and a religious one at that.

Rosalynn's one simple faith, quiet and nonflamboyant as it was, immeasurably strengthened her those first years of marriage. When the babies were bedded for the night and she felt lonely for her husband miles away on some distant ocean, Rosalynn found comfort reading from her Bible before going to sleep.

When Jimmy was on submarine duty, she was deeply grateful that, unlike some of the other wives, she always had her religion to turn to. The days were long for the wives of the men on submarines, and news of their husbands was scanty. It was always a red letter day when the USS *Pomfret* returned safely to base.

*   *   *

Jimmy returned full of tales of life at sea, and one of them was a frightening account of a sailor who went mad down under the water. Rosalynn was beginning even then to be interested in mental hygiene. The story of the unfortunate young man stayed in her mind for a long time.

She knew that an often sick Jimmy carried his vomit bucket to duty on the bridge. She knew too that the Lord had surely been with him one night when the *Pomfret* surfaced in the Pacific and Jimmy was swept into the ocean by a wave—usually a fatal experience—only to be thrown back on deck by another.

Once the *Pomfret's* radio transmitter went dead and the navy lost contact. Its crew listened morbidly to the broadcast of their own obituaries: "To all ships in the Pacific. Be on the lookout for floating debris left by submarine *USS Pomfret*, believed to have been sunk approximately 700 miles south of Midway Island."

Later, it was to his wife that Jimmy confided his reverence for the man who would become like a second father to him, Admiral Hyman Rickover, popularly called "Father of the Nuclear Navy." Rickover's constant urging of Jimmy to concentrate on nuclear physics and enginering would one day blossom far beyond the young officer's naval experience. Carter's energy and environmental views as we know them today are the direct result of his studies under Admiral Rickover.

*   *   *

Rosalynn first knew financial security as a naval wife. Her Jimmy was at the peak of his chosen career, and there was prestige enough for both of them. With Jimmy's ambitions, to say nothing of her own, he might one day rise to the rank of admiral. Then her husband was called home to his real father in Plains, who was fast losing a battle with cancer.

Father and son talked of times past during that last treasured month together. Earl Carter had often been harsh with Jimmy in his boyhood; the peach switch had never been absent. Now, at the end, they each found a new appreciation for one another, and Jimmy came to realize what that rich, red Georgia earth really meant to him.

When Earl was dying, dozens of neighbors and friends, black and white, came bearing gifts—favorite dishes, flowers from the garden, kindly words. Jimmy was surprised to see how the black workers cried when they heard the news of his father's passing—and even more so when it was revealed how Earl had helped so many of their neighbors in his own quiet way: cash to the needy, scholarships

36

for the deserving, and even graduation dresses for the school girls.

"If I died, nobody would really care, not really care," Jimmy wrote to Rosalynn back in New London.

They buried Earl beneath that great sea of marble and granite which is the cemetery at Plains.

*　　*　　*

A something long dormant was awakening in Rosalynn's husband. Miss Lillian explains it best: "He came rather late for a deep love of this land, even though he worked it with his Daddy from the time he was a small boy until he went into the Navy."

Jimmy says, "I came home from the Navy to see my Daddy die, and the thought struck me that here were my roots, here were my ancestors, these were the fields I had worked in, these are the people I grew up with . . . "

*　　*　　*

Miss Lillian had been right when she said that Jimmy had worked for his father on the farm since he was a small boy. Often he was expected to work when everybody else was having a holiday. "If all the other field workers were off for the afternoon," Jimmy explained, "and he wanted me to turn the potato vines so he could plow on Monday, Daddy would say to me, 'Hot' (he called me 'Hot-Shot'), would you like to turn the potato vines this afternoon?' And I would much rather have gone to the movies or something, but I always said, 'Yes, Sir, Daddy.' And I would do it. But he didn't have to give me many direct orders, and I never did disobey a direct order."

*　　*　　*

All the way back to New London, Jimmy's thoughts were centered on what his heart said he must do. A fellow officer remembers the mental torture that Jimmy went through: "He was really torn by that situation. It was agony. His father was the mainstay of that town, the banker and the landowner. He was a baron in a feudal situation. Jimmy had a strong sense that nobody in his family could hold it all together but him. He felt that if he didn't go back and take the burden, the town would die."

Yet to break the news to Rosalynn was another matter.

_3_

"IT was the only serious argument we ever had," says Jimmy. Rosalynn strongly resisted the move back to Plains.

"I didn't want to come home," she agrees. "I was having such a good time travelling around and being independent. He tried and tried to talk me into it, but I just wouldn't give up. I guess I was being stubborn, but I just didn't want to come home. Jimmy decided that he was going to do it anyway. There was absolutely nothing I could do about it, so I gave in."

Once settled, Jimmy called Miss Lillian in the middle of the night and said, "Mother, I have no alternative. I'm going to come home."

Sadly, Rosalynn packed up their belongings including the treasured mementoes of their life in Hawaii. There was a numbness inside as she thought of the future. Well, at least, she thought, with all the grandmothers, aunts, uncles, and cousins available, she would get some help with the children. Jeff was still only a baby.

* * *

The return of Jimmy and Rosalynn Carter to Plains, "was not," he says, "a momentous event for the community." It was 1953 when the young family settled into a $31-a-month cinderblock house in the town's only federal housing project.

Rosalynn did not nurse her disappointment for long. Just as she had always turned their apartments on bases into attractive little homes, Rosalynn did the same with her cinderblock project. Her interior decorating skills transformed the four rooms into the kind of retreat that Jimmy liked. There were reproductions of famous paintings hanging on the walls, which she had painted the soft pastel colors of her choice.

All their favorite books, some well worn with use, were neatly stacked in the bookshelves that Jimmy had made. The first thing that her mother-in-law, Miss Lillian, always did in visiting a new home was to look around for books. If there were none in evidence, she reputedly never visited that home again.

On the table, for all to see, was the Bible in which the names of their three sons were carefully recorded with a space left for that still hoped for baby girl.

She soon realized that Jimmy had been right in his feeling that he was essential to the continuation of the family peanut business. His father's generosity had made them penny poor. There were many outstanding notes that his kindness had never allowed him to collect. New organization was badly needed. Jimmy knew he could count on his wife to help in what he later called their "new life together of total sharing." "I think the relationship really started when we returned to Plains," says Rosalynn.

The first rule in having a successful business is to engage a good bookkeeper. In this case, Rosalynn appointed herself. Then she set herself the task of learning bookkeeping.

"I got textbooks on accounting from a friend, and I studied them. So, soon I could advise Jimmy on what part of the operation we were making money on and what we were losing money on. He would have to ask me."

In a short space of time, she had transformed herself from a young naval housewife into an integral part of the Carter family's vast peanut operation.

As the boys grew, they too would be encouraged to play their own small part in the business. "We've always worked together as a family," says their mother. "The children would come from school to the peanut warehouse—on Saturdays too. It drew us together. We didn't have much money; we just worked hard. The boys would be encouraged to save their earnings for their future education."

While Jimmy applied his talents to modernizing the farming methods, Rosalynn was meticulous in her own department. "As the business developed," she says, "Jimmy would come to me and say, 'Does this work; should we continue to do this in the business?' And I could advise him."

In spite of Rosalynn's devotion and careful bookkeeping, she could not control the elements. That first year saw one of the worst droughts in the history of Georgia. Red dust blew from the parched fields, clinging to storefronts and houses. Even the tombstones in Lebanon Cemetery turned red like fire. Their net income was only $254, yet together in the years that followed, they saw their peanut business grow into a million-dollar enterprise.

*   *   *

During the long winter evenings and always on weekends, they embarked once more on their chosen program of self-improvement, which surely gladdened the heart of their old high school teacher, Miss Julia Coleman. They never forgot her and, when she was sick, visited her with little gifts.

"We studied books on the great artists, on the great operas and music appreciation. And we studied those things together," Rosalynn fondly remembers. "One Christmas, Jimmy asked his mother for the complete works of Shakespeare. It was a very fulfilling life. I could never sit and drink coffee and talk about babies and clothes."

While Rosalynn read and reread Carson McCullers's *Member of the Wedding* and *The Heart Is a Lonely Hunter*, both novels about her beloved Southland, Jimmy took a liking to the poems of Dylan Thomas, the tragic Welsh poet. His favorite author remained James Agee (1909–1953), a fellow Southerner whose *Let Us Now Praise Famous Men*, which poetically and sympathetically portrays the life of poor tenant farmers grubbing out a meager living on land they could never hope to own, has become a classic.

*   *   *

Jimmy and Rosalynn saved for years to make a trip to New Orleans. There they spent hours like other tourists walking the streets of the French Quarter and exploring the ancient cemeteries. Later, when success had made life easier and they could afford a month's vacation in Mexico, Rosalynn says, "We got the Spanish book and tapes and really studied. We worked hours and hours—and when we went, we stopped in places where no English was spoken, so we *had* to use our Spanish."

Miss Allie, the family, and the people of Plains—for everybody knew everybody, including the children's pets, by name—soon had a new way of referring to Rosalynn Carter:

"One perfect rose."

_4_

SUNDAY was the Lord's Day in Plains. Rosalynn and Jimmy, then as now, would sit holding hands during the sermon. Rosalynn's family are Methodists, but upon marrying into the Carter family she adopted the Baptist faith.

Sunday morning service at the First Baptist Church highlighted the Jimmy Carters' week. With Jimmy in his navy blue suit and Rosalynn wearing neat, tailored dresses she usually made herself, they made a devoted couple with their three boys. Jimmy taught in the men's Sunday School, and for a time Rosalynn supervised a class also. There was a good deal of hymn singing, especially the old-time hymns which Jimmy and Rosalynn loved best of all.

Evangelical Christians such as the Carters place great importance on what is known as the Christian conversion experience. They believe that mankind is born in sin and bound for a literal hell unless they accept God's offer of salvation. Evangelicals are found not just among Southern Baptists, but in other denominations as well as in many social and economic levels of our society.

Rosalynn's own faith was and still is a simple one: first to be a good wife and mother; and then to leave the world a better place for having lived here. Ever since she was a small girl, she accepted Jesus Christ as her personal Saviour. With Christ, she fervidly believed, all things were possible.

*　　*　　*

Her mother-in-law, Miss Lillian, had this definition of her own role as a Christian: "I go to church on Sunday, but I don't think all churchgoers are Christians. I think there's a difference between religion and Christianity."

Asked what an Evangelical believes and what he is talking about when he speaks of being "born again," Jimmy once told a Baptist newspaper editor, "It is very difficult for anyone who has not had that experience to understand."

At the time of his own conversion experience, he felt, "If I walk across the street, no car will ever dare to hit me." *It was as simple as that.*

Rosalynn rejects the more dramatic stories about Jimmy's conversion, especially those concerning her teenage friend, now the faith-healing evangelist, Ruth Carter Stapleton: "Jimmy did talk to Ruth about her relationship with Christ, and she did have an impact on him, but there was none of this going out under the pine trees and having some kind of religious experience."

At home they enjoyed family Bible readings and what they called "circle prayer" in which the children were encouraged to name God's blessings, such as the pretty flowers, the beautiful sunset, and things like that. Sometimes they held a community prayer meeting in their living room for family and neighbors. Jimmy enjoyed teaching and preaching.

Family grace was short except on special occasions when Jimmy gave a little sermon in addition to the usual prayer,

God is great
God is good
Let us thank Him for
Our food.

*   *   *

The elegant, white frame edifice now covered with aluminum siding and known as the First Baptist Church of Plains was built in 1909. The building stands among tall trees at the end of a street of stately Victorian homes; its steeple is a landmark for miles. In a town with a population of only 683, the Baptist congregation has lavished generations of love and money on the church's rich fabrics and furnishings. It is a building of taste and refinement.

According to Deacon Ernest Turner, who with his wife June own the local hardware store on Main Street, the Gothic-style stained glass windows with their soft blues, greens and reds were thought to be of Italian origin. They were recently restored at a cost of some $2,000, says Deacon Turner. Jimmy and Rosalynn's Uncle Buddy (Alton Carter, the Carter clan's patriarch and historian who died in 1978) was always telling visitors to his son's antique shop to be sure and see "our fine church windows, as fine as any cathedral's."

The church floors are covered with deep-pile, maroon carpeting that offsets pews ornately carved with acanthus leaves, a motif much beloved in the South. The pews rise theater-like in tiers, so that at all times the pulpit and choir are visible to the congregation. On the wall hangs a notice that reads, "Whenever a church or denomination loses its concern for reaching outsiders with its message, it has already begun to die."

The church was a welcome oasis for Rosalynn and Jimmy after a week of hard work in the peanut business. "Amazing Grace," beloved of Southern churchgoers and evangelists the world over, was Jimmy's favorite hymn. The hymn's author, the Reverend John Newton (1725–1807), is described on his tombstone in Olney Churchyard, England:

Once an infidel and libertine
A servant of slaves in Africa
Was by the rich mercy of Our Lord and Saviour
Jesus Christ
Preserved, restored, pardoned
And appointed to preach the faith
He had long labored to destroy.

*   *   *

Through the happy 1950s, Rosalynn, with her simple hair style and neat drip-dry suits, watched proudly as their family business prospered. It seemed like a miracle, what Jimmy and she had accomplished working together as a team. She realized now just how right he had been in coming home to Plains.

With the advent of the turbulent 1960s, talk of racial integration was on every tongue. All Plains knew Miss Lillian's tolerant views concerning blacks. They had never forgotten how she once served coffee to the student son of a respected black bishop. Her so-called radical views of equality were shared by her eldest son.

As a child in rural Archery, Jimmy had as his best friend a black, A. D. Davis, now a sawmill worker with a large family. With her own small brood, Miss Lillian defiantly took A. D. along for Saturday afternoon movies in Americus. She was not the sort to leave anybody out. However, in the segregated public school and in the First Baptist Church, all Jimmy's friends were, of necessity, white.

*   *   *

Rosalynn supported her husband's unpopular stand on integration. It was not an easy decision for they both had much to lose. Even their hard-earned business was threatened both by economic sanctions and bombing.

Bothered by the local White Citizens Council, who, tiring of Jimmy's refusal to join their fight to retain segregated schools, even offered to pay his dues. Jimmy's reply was characteristic of the man: "I've got five dollars and I'd flush it down the toilet before I'd give it to you."

When Plains Baptist Church voted to keep out the blacks, Miss Lillian remembers how Jimmy's "vein in his temple that throbs when he's mad was really going that morning."

Standing before the hushed congregation, his voice broke with emotion as he declared, "Before we vote I've got to tell you how I feel. This is God's House, not ours. How can we stand in the doorway and tell God's people they cannot come into His house?"

His plea fell on stony ground, for only six members voted to let their black brethren in. They were Rosalynn and Jimmy, Miss Lillian, Jack, Chip, and one other.

Rosalynn personally took much of the scurrilous abuse aimed at her family for their dedicated stand on civil rights. Both at the warehouse and in her home, she received terrible phone calls, many threatening and obscene. Although their home was threatened with firebombing at a time when black homes and churches were being burned throughout the Deep South, Rosalynn Carter stood firm. Close friends say she showed real courage, verbally rebuking her antagonists.

Middle son Chip, in recalling those anxious times, says, "We were all taught at a very early age that everybody was equal. We had the only liberal parents in Plains, and I guess I suffered. I used to get in fights every day at school. I had to come home at lunch and change shirts!"

As for Miss Lillian, she had been called "nigger lover" too often to get really ruffled. Her fellow matrons in Plains had been horrified when she headed the local campaign to elect Lyndon B. Johnson to the presidency. Johnson was considered a traitor in the South because of his role in the passage of the Civil Rights Act.

Rosalynn and Miss Lillian both shared experiences like that of Lady Bird Johnson when she arrived in Charleston, South Carolina, in the campaign train, *The Lady Bird Special*. Mrs. Johnson was openly snubbed by little old ladies who slammed their window shutters in her face. The city, said Lady Bird, whose mother was the cultured Minnie Lee Pattillo of Billingsley, Alabama, "looked like an exquisite corpse."

_ 5 _

OVER the years as bookkeeper at the Carter Peanut Warehouse, Rosalynn's skill with figures increased so much that she quite intended to sit for the CPA examination. She never did, for, in a way, history was repeating itself. She never mailed her final college entry papers because of Jimmy Carter, and it was because of him again that she never sat for the accountancy tests.

Jimmy had decided to go into politics.

Perhaps she had sensed it for a long time, had noticed how he enjoyed standing outside the Baptist church giving his little spiel. Both Jimmy and Rosalynn were highly moral people. They now believed that he had a special mission to serve his fellow men.

"I had to manage the business three months a year when Jimmy was away in the state legislature," says Rosalynn, "and I felt very, very important, because he couldn't have done it at all if I hadn't managed the business."

With Rosalynn taking charge of all his campaign correspondence, Jimmy ran on the Democratic ticket for the Georgia Senate in 1962 and won. Nobody was more proud than she, with the exception of his mother, Miss Lillian, of course. When Jimmy's father died, Miss Lillian was offered his senate seat, but tactfully refused it.

Rosalynn hated the separation, but Atlanta was not far away. Unlike the days when he was away on submarine duty, she did know where he could be found.

Noting his sincerity, Senate old-timers jokingly referred to Jimmy Carter as "stubborn as a South Georgia turtle." Nor did his passion for hard work and long hours go unnoticed by his fellow senators. He worked five instead of four days a week, returning to Plains on the weekends.

On Saturdays they were like two newlyweds, cooking breakfast and supper together. "He is a better cook than me," Rosalynn once said of her Jimmy's culinary efforts.

Their boys were growing up nicely; like their parents, they did not smoke or drink. Jeff spent much of his leisure time playing ball with the sons of Bill and Ida English. "He was here every weekday," says Bill, "and was like one of our own." Jimmy and Rosalynn liked him home at weekends, which was very much a family time for them."

Bill is an expert on the installation of hotel sprinklers, and his work takes him around the country. Miss Ida is devoted to Rosalynn and Jimmy. When she was buying a lot from Jimmy on which to build the family home, he insisted on letting them have three lots because as, he put it, "growing boys needed room to play."

*   *   *

"Jimmy took to politics like a duck to water," old Uncle Alton Carter told me. It was Alton who described the young Rosalynn as "neat, pretty, clean, smart, reserved, and not a blab-mouth or high roller."

Alton's nephew enjoyed his days in the state Senate so much that, with Rosalynn's approval, he decided to run for the post of Governor of Georgia. With a supreme effort, Rosalynn rose above her natural shyness to become his most loyal campaigner, a role she has never relinquished.

"We had a long talk," Rosalynn says, "and Jimmy convinced me that he knew I could do it."

Unfortunately Jimmy lost the election, finishing third, which was a great disappointment because the winner was Lester Maddox, a segregationist whose views were completely opposite to his own. "To lose is one thing," Rosalynn was quoted as saying at the time, "but to lose to Lester Maddox!"

Rosalynn accompanied Jimmy on a much needed vacation by the sea after which, according to his sister, Gloria Carter Spann, "he came home talking about the shrimp boats, went down to the office, and started talking about the next campaign."

First, however, there was one prior engagement to fulfill for his God. Accepting a call from the Southern Baptist Convention, Jimmy took part in a missionary program among one hundred families in Pennsylvania, among whom there were no acknowledged Christian believers. The experience proved a turning point in his life. According to Rosalynn, "He called me at home one day and said that he had just put himself completely in God's hands. He was witnessing at the time with a man from Texas who had done this every year, and he was in his seventies."

* * *

Rosalynn and Jimmy's vacation by the sea proved to be a real second honeymoon, for nine months afterwards, on October 19, 1967, their longed for baby girl was born. There was great rejoicing, and they named her "Amy Lynn," a name which Miss Lillian, who had astounded Plains by joining the Peace Corps at 68, wrote from India to say that she liked.

Rosalynn's younger sister, Allethea, had lost her own baby through a miscarriage. "When Amy was born," says

Allethea, "Rosalynn told me, 'Consider Amy your child, too.' "

Rosalynn, who was past 40, had been unable to conceive since the birth of Jeff, fifteen years before. Then the doctors discovered that she had a cyst on an ovary and successfully removed it. Then came that second honeymoon and the miracle pregnancy.

Amy Lynn was their living proof that God answers prayers. From the beginning she was a beautiful child who, said Rosalynn, "in a way had four fathers." She meant Jimmy and the three boys. The Four Fathers wept openly when Rosalynn and baby Amy were wheeled out of the hospital delivery room.

*　　*　　*

In 1970 Jimmy again ran for governor, and this time he won. Rosalynn completely overcame her initial shyness to public speaking. She was particularly good at addressing women's groups. When things were difficult, she displayed a sense of calm inherited from her mother, Miss Allie.

"I think the worst thing that ever happened to Rosalynn," says sister-in-law Gloria, "was when she was handing out brochures and a man spat on her. She went right on as if nothing had happened."

Under fire and the excitement of a political campaign Rosalynn was finding a new confidence. Again she was more than proving that she could be, as she termed it, "a partner with my husband." Little Amy, then a chubby, fair-headed toddler, was beside her as she proudly watched Jimmy be sworn in as Georgia's seventy-sixth governor.

In his inaugural speech, the new Governor Carter declared: "At the end of a long campaign, I believe I know the people of this state as well as anyone. Based on this knowledge of Georgians, north and south, rural and urban, liberal and conservative, I say to you quite frankly that the time for racial discrimination is over. Our people have already made this major and difficult decision, but we cannot underestimate the challenge of hundreds of minor decisions yet to be made. Our inherent human charity and our religious beliefs will be taxed to the limit. No poor, rural, weak, or black person should ever have to bear the additional burden of being deprived of the opportunity of an education, a job, or simple justice."

With all her heart, Rosalynn Carter believed in Jimmy's words. They had gone over the speech many times together, for Jimmy always has been the kind of man to prefer his own words to those of a paid speechwriter.

Later, as they drove in an open limousine through throngs of cheering Georgians, Rosalynn felt a deep sense of thankfulness. With Amy sitting on her father's knee, many in the crowd were reminded of the never-to-be-forgotten young Kennedys—Jack, Jackie, Caroline, and young John-John.

*   *   *

In December 1970, their beloved Mary Fitzpatrick came into the Jimmy Carter family. Mary was engaged by Georgia's new First Lady to become Amy's nanny, and the position was to be part of Mary's rehabilitation program.

Mary had been sentenced to life in prison following her conviction for a murder she was alleged to have committed at Lumpkin, Georgia. The murder occurred when Mary and her cousin, Aniemaude Perry, went to a bar and Aniemaude and another woman got into a fight over Aniemaude's gun. Mary tried to intervene and the gun went off killing the woman's boyfriend. The woman swore that Mary had shot him. Although Mary declared her innocence in a tearful plea, she was sentenced to life imprisonment.

Born into a poverty-stricken black family, Mary's life was one of tragedy. She cannot remember her own father, and a stepfather ran off when she was 9. Her older sister, Carrie Frances, a happy, lively youngster, died of an abcess on the brain when she was 12. Mary wonders if, with better medical attention, Carrie Frances might have been saved.

At the early age of 14, Mary married and gave birth to a boy, Lonnie. The marriage broke up shortly afterwards, and Mary went to live in New York City, where another son, David Jerome, was born. The boys, both well-mannered and studious, live with Mary's younger sister, Gloria, in Atlanta.

*   *   *

Mary traveled to Atlanta to visit Mrs. Carter. She was extremely nervous, wondering how the Carters would like her. Rosalynn and Mary took to each other at once. As for Amy, she was delighted with her new nanny, although she sometimes cried when Mary had to leave for the night. Mary would sing all the old-time spirituals to the child; "Swing Low, Sweet Chariot" was Amy's favorite.

"Please Mary, answer," she would beg when the two played hide and seek in the long corridors of the splendid Governor's Mansion. Under Mary's supervision, Amy baked tiny biscuits for her father. For both nanny and child, it was the beginning of a very special and rewarding relationship. Rosalynn has always been noted for being a shrewd judge of character, and Mary Fitzpatrick has never let her down.

Mary in time became so much a part of the family that she borrowed books from the Carter's precious library. Those dealing with history and politics were her favorites. When she came upon something that she could not understand, Rosalynn and Jimmy were never too busy to explain it.

*   *   *

As First Lady of Georgia and its official hostess, Rosalynn, a Leo, take-charge person, found herself running the million-dollar mansion with its staff of fourteen. There was a great deal of entertaining, which included many public figures on official visits to the state.

She became a familiar figure digging in the garden with the state prison trustees who maintained the grounds beautifully. She took a keen interest in the publishing of a book about the Governor's Mansion and says rather modestly, "It wasn't as elaborate as the one Jackie did at the White House, but we made enough money to redo the mansion's formal garden."

*   *   *

Her First Lady role did not make Rosalynn overly fashion conscious. With a size-eight figure that many women her age have a right to envy, she still preferred the conservative styles that suited her.

Once, during this period, she described her wardrobe shopping this way: "If anybody is coming up from home [Plains] or Americus, they send me a box of clothes to try on. If I like them, I keep them. I hate shopping. I have never had designer clothes because they cost too much." There were two dress shops in Americus.

The frugal days following the death of her father when she was only 13 had left an indelible mark on the rest of her life. Money was hard to come by and must never be wasted.

"When Jimmy was elected and all of a sudden he was Governor, I woke up one morning, thinking, 'You've got to be perfect all the time. Amy, and she was only 3, has to be perfect all the time.' It took us about four months to realize you just can't live like that. Besides, clothes don't mean that much to me."

Rosalynn continued to select the new Governor's suits from Cohen's store in Americus. He also hated doing his own shopping. Rosalynn, then as now, prefers seeing him wear gray or blue. "Jimmy," she says, "doesn't care."

*　　*　　*

As First Lady of Georgia she quickly realized she could now promote her favorite projects, particularly in the field of mental health. Two members of the Carter family had been hospitalized for psychiatric problems, and Rosalynn felt compassion not only for them, but for others similarly afflicted.

Madeline MacBean, Jimmy's secretary, recalls that Rosalynn "talked to the Governor about the lack of mental retardation facilities in the state, and he created a commission to study it. . . . Rosalynn was on that commission [the Governor's Commission to improve Service for the Mentally and Emotionally Handicapped], and she personally visited every facility in the state. She was shocked at what she saw."

Rosalynn's philosophy became "You do what you have to do." As a result of the Commission's recommendations, great reforms were made in Georgia's state mental retardation programs.

Because his wife cared, Governor Carter was encouraged to do more than any of his predecessors for the mentally ill. When he was first elected to office, his native state had no community mental health centers. Four years later when his term expired there were fourteen federally funded centers and one hundred smaller "satellite" centers. Says Mary King, who became President Carter's adviser on women's issues in Washington, "Mrs. Carter was directly responsible for getting them."

Rosalynn was honorary chairman of the Georgia Special Olympics for Retarded Children. From 1974, she served as a voting delegate from the Georgia Association for Mental Health to the National Mental Health Association's annual meeting and a member of its Board of Directors.

When she was campaigning to win her husband the governorship, women would walk up and ask, "What will he do to help me with my retarded child if he's elected?" Later Rosalynn asked Jimmy, "Why do they tell me about their problems?"

"Because you might be the only person they'll ever see who may be close to somebody who can help them," was his reply.

And help they did.

*   *   *

To gain first-hand experience among those suffering from mental sickness, Rosalynn became an ordinary volunteer worker at the Georgia Regional Hospital in Atlanta. There she visited ward patients, sold candy in the gift shop, made follow-up calls to patients, and even shampooed their hair.

Barbara Sugarman, Georgia's Director of Volunteer Services, wryly admits that "There was only one thing I couldn't get her to do. She had learned the hula in Hawaii and really knew how to do it, so I asked her to perform for the talent show one year, but she talked Jimmy into reading 'Twas the Night before Christmas' instead!"

*   *   *

As Miss Allie says so often of her famous daughter, "She can be real saving at times," and never was this more true than during her sojourn in the Governor's Mansion. Both Carters were angry at the amount of water, to say nothing of the money, it cost to water the mansion's lawns. Jimmy complained that there was too much extra toilet tissue in his bathroom. Cattle were allowed to graze in the State Hospital grounds to keep down the expense of cutting the grass.

If Rosalynn was particularly saving, then Jimmy was noted for being the hardest and most Spartan worker in his own executive organization. William Harper, his former legal counsel, said at the time, "He had his driver bring him from the mansion, twenty miles away, to the office, and he'd read memos in the car. He was always there by 7:15 AM. Then he'd have one cup of coffee, never more, and read the morning papers."

*　　*　　*

Jimmy's work routine was broken by the most simple form of relaxation, one that he had enjoyed in childhood; the collecting of old bottles. With a favorite dump in nearby Griffin, he patiently shoveled dirt and debris until he found the much prized old patent medicine and early Coke bottles he was looking for. These would be taken back to the Governor's Mansion where an always enthusiastic Rosalynn would help wash them. In time they were added to his large collection installed on the sturdy wooden shelves he had built to house them in the family home at Plains.

Rosalynn also saw to it that Jimmy made time for another favorite hobby and one that his mother loved also—fishing.

Governor Jimmy Carter is also on record for his personal sighting of a UFO. This he meticulously reported to the proper authorities.

During Rosalynn's first year as First Lady of Georgia, she entertained seven hundred and fifty dinner guests each week for eight weeks. Betty Ford, the First Lady of the United States, was a well-remembered guest who thoroughly enjoyed the Carters' family-style entertaining.

Of those days, Rosalynn notes, "At the Governor's Mansion I thought I had to be very sophisticated and serve fancy dinners. You don't have to do that. Guests want to eat the food we eat. It was whatever I'm comfortable with."

Says Irene Horne, a friend of Rosalynn's from college days, "Once when some big shots from Germany were visiting the Governor's Mansion, Rosalynn, who had just taken a cooking course, told me, 'If I were in Germany, I would want to eat plain, German cooking.' So, even though this was a very formal dinner, Rosalynn served them Southern cooking, with sweet potatoes and collards . . . and they loved it!"

However, Rosalynn only served wine—no hard liquor— in the Governor's Mansion. "It saved money," she says. "I didn't have to have bartenders."

_6_

MISS Lillian, who had returned home from India, was staying in the Governor's Mansion recuperating from a broken shoulder. One evening Jimmy walked into her room and announced, "Mama, I'm going to run for President."

"President of what?" she asked him.

Jimmy cannot remember any specific "scene" in his family life with Rosalynn when he first made the great decision to run. "It was," he says, "a slow realization during 1972 when I met the other candidates for president and when I had also met my first President, Richard Nixon."

Meanwhile Rosalynn had confided to their sons about Jimmy's possible candidacy: "My boys and I decided that Jimmy knew a lot more about a lot of things than did these men who were running for President."

Rosalynn had watched them all come and go at the Governor's Mansion. She had served them dinner and welcomed them as overnight guests. Besides President Nixon, George Wallace, Nelson Rockefeller, Ronald Reagan, Henry Jackson, Edmund Muskie, George McGovern, and Hubert Humphrey had all passed through her door. Rosalynn with her own quiet grass-roots sense had assessed them all and had found them wanting.

In October 1974, Jimmy publicly hinted that he might decide to be a candidate for the Democrats in 1976. On December 12, he officially announced that he would indeed seek his party's nomination.

Most political writers simply dismissed his credibility as a national contender. Even his own state's largest newspaper, the *Atlanta Journal-Constitution*, in screaming headlines demanded to know:

JIMMY CARTER IS RUNNING FOR WHAT?

*   *   *

Jimmy's term as governor ended on January 14, 1975. From that moment the Carter presidential campaign was off to a good start with Rosalynn playing a vital role. While Jimmy put in an eighteen-hour workday, she made her own plans to bring the husband she loved to the people. "My secret weapon" was the way Jimmy described her.

Rosalynn recalls that she and Edna Langford, Jack Carter's mother-in-law, "just got in the car and drove." Descending on small towns hat beckoned them with radio or television towers, Rosalynn would announce to the sometimes startled station directors, "I'm here; please interview me now."

*   *   *

Rosalynn often looks back on those early campaign days: "I call Edna when I'm feeling depressed or need a boost . . . She was with me starting with the primaries, when I had no one else."

Rosalynn's simple strategy was to familiarize people with Jimmy in areas where they had never heard of him.

"I'm Mrs. Jimmy Carter," she would introduce herself, all the time smiling through those gray-green eyes. "My husband is running for President."

More often than not she would elicit Miss Lillian's response: "President of what?"

*   *   *

On the Carter homefront, Amy was now living with her paternal grandmother, Miss Lillian. Rosalynn always tried to return to Plains for spiritual and physical replenishment on weekends.

Amy's much-loved nanny, Mary Fitzpatrick, had returned to prison when Jimmy's governorship ended. It was a terrible wrench for both Mary and Amy. When she had to say good-bye, Mary remembers how Amy screamed.

Busy as she now was launching Jimmy's presidential campaign, Rosalynn never deserted Mary. She found time to visit her both at the Fulton County Jail and at the Atlanta Work Release Center, where Mary went as a cook later in 1975.

Criticized for leaving 8-year-old Amy for what would amount to some eighteen months of campaign travel, Rosalynn said that Amy was happy staying with her grandmothers, Miss Lillian and Miss Allie. She was also surrounded by numerous cousins and schoolfriends.

*   *   *

With Jimmy's blessing, "Just ask the Lord to help you do the best you can, and you'll do alright," Rosalynn Carter set out to conquer the hearts of America.

In her conservative black pumps and pulling her luggage on a small wheel attachment behind her, she became a familiar figure at the larger airports. Finally, as election day drew close, she would fly with her own staff in on one of two whispering Learjets. Rosalynn Smith Carter, called by some the "Steel Magnolia" had come a long way.

Of her efforts, she modestly said, "I believe that anybody could do what I've done. I never dreamed I'd be in the Governor's Mansion. I never thought I could make a speech, but you just do it. I believe I was helped by the fact of feeling secure, of having the kind of stability that comes from knowing all those people in Plains cared for me."

"At first I worried about everything I said, how I looked; was I dressed just right. But you cannot do that and be effective, so I learned from Jimmy that you just relax and do the best you can."

She earned the reputation of being her husband's closest campaign adviser. At the end of the day, it was she who shared his thoughts and ambitions.

"I have very strong opinions about everything and I always let Jimmy know how I feel," she admitted during those tiring days. "He doesn't always react well to everything. But there are very few things Jimmy decides that we don't talk about."

Of Rosalynn, Jimmy said, "She operates independently from me. She helps form my positions because she has a sensitive way of understanding what other people feel. Also, she is able to get a much more frank and unbiased expression of criticism from people than I can. They can approach Rosalynn and say, 'I think Jimmy ought to do this' or 'He's hurting himself when he fails to do this.' So, in every possible way she's a full partner or better." This was his way of paying his wife the highest of compliments.

When a five o'clock commuter in Chicago's North Western Station yelled, "Are you running for First Lady?" Rosalynn looked him in the eye, drew her slim body poker straight and replied almost defiantly:

"Yes."

Before he had time to recover from her answer, she spoke again: "There are so many things to be done in this country; so much in mental health and for the elderly. It excites me to think that I could help."

She paused for breath, and the man demanded, "How can you justify that your promises have anything to do with Jimmy Carter's campaign?"

Rosalynn smiled sweetly and stated, somewhat demurely, in her best Southern belle tradition, "I come with him."

*   *   *

Repeatedly, she echoed Jimmy's most dominant theme—that the American people "have lost trust in the government in Washington," that "Jimmy Carter can restore that trust."

Her workdays stretched sometimes to thirteen and fourteen hours. Her aides marvelled at her energy, especially since she had come so late in life to political campaigning.

A typical three-day program included visiting eight cities, giving fourteen addresses to varying audiences, including women's church groups, seven news conferences, twelve magazine and newspaper interviews, and at least ten television appearances.

In addition, there were always local Democratic and labor leaders to meet, plus ceremonial public appearances. City mayors and their wives would turn out in style to greet her.

Jackie Kennedy had been called the "American Princess." Rosalynn Carter was following in her footsteps.

*   *   *

With Jimmy, Rosalynn took a short much-needed break to give Amy a day of sightseeing in Washington, D.C., where hopefully they would make their home for the next few years. Strolling through leafy Lincoln Park they looked like other tourists. Amy was much impressed that she might one day soon be living in the White House.

*　　*　　*

Rosalynn had active support from other members of the Carter family who in one week alone visited some ninety-seven cities in twenty-five states.

Miss Lillian's younger sister, Mrs. Emily Dolvin, a widow, known in the family as "Aunt Sissy," became a one-woman Carter Armada. From Georgia to Maine she turned up to greet voters with, "Hi, I'm Jimmy Carter's Aunt Sissy. I hope you'll vote for my boy as President."

Particularly popular with senior citizen groups, Aunt Sissy was not above gamely milking her first cow in La Crosse, Wisconsin, if it made local headlines for Jimmy. Which it did, plus some equally favorable national ones as well. Aunt Sissy milked that cow with Southern style.

Jeff Carter, Jimmy and Rosalynn's youngest son, made his own solo tour of the Midwest. They loved his cowboy boots and tight blue jeans in Oklahoma. "I give speeches, I eat cookies, I cut ribbons," said the Carter who had best inherited his father's smile.

Rosalynn's own most annoying experience on the road was the day her luggage was stolen. She only had the clothes she stood up in. Most women who could afford it would have dashed out and bought a new wardrobe. Not Rosalynn Carter. For several nights she washed out her single outfit in the hotel bedroom sink. She always looked spick-and-span next morning.

*   *   *

Back to Plains for weekends, Rosalynn enjoyed the privacy of her own kitchen with its familiar furnishings, polka dot curtains, bright red coffee pot and matching pans, and copper cooking utensils with elaborate, black, wrought-iron handles.

There, on Saturday evenings, Jimmy would fry the eggplant and squash, fresh picked from their garden, while Rosalynn prepared the rest of the supper.

To see such domesticity was to recall Rosalynn's remark, "I just love to cook, sew, iron shirts, and pick beans straight from the garden."

*   *   *

Mr. and Mrs. Jimmy Carter publicly listed their finances, as of December 31, 1975, as follows:

Assets $819,268
Net Worth $811,983
Liabilities (For notes and accounts payable) $7,285
Income (declared on joint federal tax return for 1975, including net of $119,244 from Carter's Warehouse)$136,139

The assets included their home in Plains, valued at $54,090. The Carter House is a sprawling, red brick ranch type set among seasoned hickory and oak trees. There is a lot of shade. Rosalynn helped design both house and garden, and they do credit to her common-sense planning. Miss Allie helped wallpaper the living room, and Rosalynn did the indoor painting herself. Jimmy designed and built the chaise on the sun porch and most of the book shelves.

Rosalynn's enjoyment of her weekends away from campaigning included trips to Walter's Grocery in a battery-

66

powered golf cart complete with a fringed canopy. On one such excursion, a barefoot Army sits beside her very involved in a large hardbound copy of the *Peanuts*. Secret Service agents, newspaper people, and tourists are everywhere, and cameras are much in evidence.

Inside the store, it is hard for Rosalynn to concentrate on her purchases. She smiles graciously, waving a hand to the crowd staring through the window. Her wedding band flashes when it catches the afternoon light.

Then she is back in the golf cart and off in the direction of home. She stops at the old railroad depot, now her husband's campaign headquarters and, telling Amy to guard the two packages of groceries, runs nimbly up the steps to disappear inside.

Amy gazes up at the platform as if expecting to see her grandmother who likes to hold court up there in her rocking chair, but it is empty. She takes a quick look at the groceries, leaps off the cart, and jumps onto a slick Western Flyer bicycle all dolled up with bright yellow reflectors. Crowds and photographers are unprepared for Amy's quicksilver actions and scatter left and right as she rides a figure eight right through their middle. Then she is back on the cart yelling "Mama" with what breath she has left.

"Mama, let's go."

Mama reappears once more, still smiling that Mona Lisa smile, which remains an enigma to many. Back in the cart beside Amy, she waves a quick good-bye to the crowd, who clap and cheer, and then they are off again on the short drive home to Woodland Avenue. They drive past the Secret Service barricades and vanish into the trees.

*   *   *

During those preelection months, weekends were always exciting and lively in Plains. With the chance of seeing

Jimmy and Rosalynn in person, the crowds grew bigger. Busloads of school children arrived; Boy and Girl Scouts walked about in uniform; and dozens of ladies in colorful pant-suits descended on the little town.

While children sold tiny bags of peanuts for a dollar each, peanut-flavored ice cream was served in a rambling ice cream parlor complete with working propeller fans suspended from the metal, embossed ceiling.

Makeshift buses and a gaily painted tour train that seemed to have escaped from Disneyland showed Carter family "historic sights" for a fee. Souvenirs were on sale everywhere, even "Jimmy dolls" complete with generous rows of teeth. Only Turner's Hardware refused to change its ways, and its trade was seemingly unhurt by the decision. A psalm was stuck to the store window, and stickers attached to the brown glaze teapots and blue spackle-ware coffee pots, proclaimed to the world: "Ernest and June Turner: The Store That Did Not Change."

*   *   *

June Turner has one of those beautiful moon-shaped faces so beloved of 1940 movie fans. Blessed with a remarkable memory for faces and a pleasing disposition, she is the epitome of what a Southern lady should be. She often holds the customers' babies while they browse in the store.

June and Ernest are concerned that Plains will become a tourist trap. That was why they refused to change the nature of Turner's Hardware and sell souvenirs like the other stores in Plains.

"Plains is a farmers' town," muses Ernest, smiling benevolently over his spectacles. "It still needs hardware and dry goods."

Business increased when a wire story reported how Secret Service agents were buying bib overalls to wear

68

"unobserved" in the crowds. "But their shiny shoes were a dead giveaway," Ernest chuckles.

Now he gets mail orders for Liberty overalls from all over the country including a Galveston Texas man who shoes horses and takes a size 52–34! Of living in Plains, Ernest Turner says philosophically, "When my neighbor's dog dies, I sympathize with him."

*　　*　　*

In front of Main Street is a stretch of wild land, old railroad tracks overgrown with creeping purple-red thyme and tiny yellow wild flowers. There is a white concrete seat and the plinth of a birdbath whose top is missing.

When night falls over Plains, all is quiet save for the chirping of a million crickets and happy black voices coming from the Skylight Club. White mists rise over Choctahatchee Creek. Lights still burn in the sprawling house off Woodland Drive.

Jimmy and Rosalynn Carter, having eaten their eggplant and squash, are fervently discussing next week's election campaign strategy.

_7_

ROSALYNN and Jimmy interrupted their hectic schedule long enough to attend the thirty-fifth anniversary of the Plains High School Class of '41. It was held at the Great Western Inn in Americus, twenty-one of the twenty-three surviving members of the class had arrived for the occasion. It was unlike any of the earlier reunions. This time one of their own was running for President of the United States. Rosalynn had arranged a similar earlier anniversary party for the Class of '41 in the Governor's Mansion.

Of Jimmy and Rosalynn's early teachers, the memorable Miss Julia Coleman had died. Her former students had many kind things to say of her that night. Rosalynn and Jimmy's first grade teacher, Mrs. Eleanor Forest, a widow, lives out her well-earned retirement in a white house in Plains, which has been her home since she too was a first grader. Miss Eleanor recalls little Jimmy Carter: "I remember Jimmy as a good student and co-operative. I can't say he was the smartest boy I've ever taught as I've taught a lot of smart boys, but he was among the top ten. I was a stern teacher. There wasn't a room big enough to hold me and a child who wouldn't mind.

"Jimmy was one of the sweetest little boys, but you can't tell much at that age. He came to school one day and said: 'Miss Eleanor, I am going to bring you my mother's diamond ring. Daddy will get her another one.'

"Jimmy is such a hard worker, and he's so determined. I think he's going to work just as hard as President as he did in school."

Miss Eleanor remembers Rosalynn as a shy but smiling girl with the largest bow of ribbon in her hair. "She was neat and meticulous in everything she did. There was never a thumbprint on any paper that she handed in."

*   *   *

Rosalynn sat proudly beside Jimmy at the main table. His new blue tie, overprinted with red buffalo, the old school emblem, drew plenty of comments. Several of the women present wanted to know if Rosalynn had chosen it.

Some of the men had grown fat and bald in the thirty-five years since high school days. Jimmy seemed to have changed least of all. He could still be easily recognized from his high school picture.

Somebody commented that of all of them present he seemed to have made the most money. Others said openly that he had married the prettiest girl in Plains. Like Jimmy she had seemingly aged least of all. A rather plump gentleman came right out and said, "That Jimmy Carter had all the luck."

One by one the graduates of '41 stood to introduce themselves, describing their present home town if they had left Plains, occupation, number of children and grandchildren. Said one woman somewhat nostalgically: "We have been close, and I guess we'll always be close. In school, one person's joy was everyone's joy; one person's sorrow was everyone's sorrow."

                              *   *   *

The reunion included five Georgia peanut farmers, a cor-
rections officer from Washington, and a man who saw fit to
confess, "All of you know how lazy I was. Well, I still am.
I married a woman with children of her own so I didn't
have to do any of the work."

Then there was the good-looking blond who said she was
secretary to a Superior Court judge. At that point Jimmy
interrupted. "Can you type? " he asked. The question was
greeted with peals of laughter. Rosalynn turned red. "Now
Jimmy," she said.

When it was Jimmy's turn to speak, even Rosalynn won-
dered what was coming next. With tongue in cheek and
grinning, the presidential candidate said, "My name is
Jimmy Carter and I'm semiretired. My family, though, is
in the lemonade stand business. [Amy had been selling lemonade to the tourists.] I have four children and one grandchild. Let me tell you about Jason. He's just the finest
grandchild that ever was born in Georgia."

                              *   *   *

Awards were then presented to the one with least hair,
the one most difficult to locate, and the one who had travelled the furthest distance to attend that evening. Former
Governor Jimmy Carter was the recipient of a red, white,
and blue hand-knitted afghan all ready for the cold Washington, D.C., winters. He was obviously touched.

Then with Rosalynn watching proudly, Jimmy rose to
speak again, this time from the heart. He recalled Miss Julia's introducing them all to the pleasures of art and liter-
ature. "I remember those debates she made us have every
Friday, and I remember how we always dreaded preparing
for them. And I remember, too, how we always liked
them."

Several eyes, Rosalynn's included, became tearful as he continued. "We had a code of our own. It prepared us to go out into the world and do the best we could. We're small and isolated down here in Plains, but you can learn just as much coming to Plains as you can from any of the people in New York City. We lived together, played together, and fought together. Now, don't any of you get too far from me. I want you to write me a letter, so I can always know where you're at. I depend on you. You are my closest friends."

He then invited them, on Rosalynn and his own behalf, to attend the next reunion at the White House, for like everyone in Plains he was confident of victory in the end.

To conclude the festivities, Lottie Tanner, the reunion's capable organizer, read her own little speech:

"I have been talking to a lot of reporters; some with cameras, some with movie picture cameras, some just with pencil and notebooks, and they have all been swell. I have tried to tell them everything I know about Jimmy and everything I can remember. They all said I have done swell. I want it to be nice in Washington, D.C., and of course, I want them to be nice to Jimmy and Rosalynn when they go there."

Then methodically folding her paper, Lottie Tanner asked, "How many of you are staying over for Sunday?" There was a great show of hands.

"Well, that's fine," she said. "I can't think of any nicer way to close our high school reunion than if we all go to church tomorrow morning with Jimmy. I'll even go and I'm a Methodist."

Poor Jimmy. He took a quick despairing glance at Rosalynn. Bone tired from campaigning, he had planned to go fishing next day.

He stood up. "Wait a minute everybody, I have a confession to make. I wasn't planning on going to church tomorrow morning, but let's see. Are a lot of you really planning to stay over and come to church?"

Again the hands shot up. Jimmy gazed at the sea of smiling faces. Then, turning to Rosalynn with a look of resignation, he conceded, "Okay, then I'll stay, and we'll all go to church."

He spoke briefly to an aide.

"You'll take care of it, won't you?"

The man looked upwards, then nodded that he would.

*   *   *

Outside in the warm Southern night, hand in hand, Rosalynn and Jimmy walked to their car. Then he waved the Secret Service driver aside, took over the wheel, and, like any other peanut farmer after an evening out, drove his wife safely back home.

_8_

EVEN with Rosalynn and Jimmy campaigning for the presidency, there were still thousands who asked, "Jimmy who?"

Interest snowballed in the Carter family roots—who they were and where they came from. The White House had no genealogical department, so, at their suggestion, I sought out the patriarch and historian of the clan, the late Alton Carter, Uncle Buddy. Then a nimble 88, he was busy with customers in the antique shop owned by his son, Senator Hugh Carter. The shop is on the main street of Plains.

With his shirt sleeves rolled up to the elbows, Alton Carter could have passed for a much younger man. He had been gifted with one of those rare photogenic minds, and he remembered me from my single previous visit a year before. "I only searched back as far as Wiley Carter," he began with a twinkle in his eye. "He shot a man."

Still recovering from this rather startling piece of information concerning the would-be President's ancestor, I watched Uncle Alton as he disappeared through some swinging doors. He reemerged a few moments later with glossy photographs of Wiley's grave in the old family cemetery, of which Alton was custodian. There were also pictures of Wiley's abandoned farm in Ellaville, Georgia, and another of Uncle Alton and nephew Jimmy looking over some family tombstones.

Uncle Alton was obviously proud of Wiley (1798–1864), a wealthy plantation owner who shot a man named Usry whom he had accused of stealing a slave. In the jury trial that followed, a witness said, "Usry and Carter were cursing each other, and both raised their guns at about the same time, and Carter fired."

Wiley Carter was found not guilty but, as an aftermath of the murder, moved his family to within twenty miles of Plains. His grave is the chief attraction in the tiny family cemetery, with its gray table tombs reminiscent of England from whence the Carter forebears came. A giant magnolia tree shades the grave now enclosed by a hideous wire-mesh fence. Two sensuous looking turtle doves are carved forever into a marble obelisk.

*   *   *

Old Alton's long life had itself been touched with violence. As a boy of 15, he witnessed the murder of his own father, William Archibald Carter (1858–1903), in a dispute over, of all mundane objects, an office desk. William, owner of three sawmills, had rented a store to a certain Will Taliaferro who, upon moving to another location, saw fit to take the desk with him. William went after the desk, and Taliaferro pulled out a pistol and shot Alton's father in the back of the head. He died next day.

William's own father, Littleberry Walker Carter (1832–1873), who had survived the War between the States, fighting of course with the Confederate Army, was stabbed to death by his business partner, D. P. McCann. The murder occurred during a drunken brawl over the takings from a home-made merry-go-round, known locally as a Flying Jenny, which the two men jointly owned. Littleberry Walker Carter's wife, Mary Ann, collapsed with shock upon hearing of her husband's death and died the same day. Indicted for murder, McCann ran off to South America and was never heard from again.

The Carter family saga for this period of its history could easily have supplied material for a Tennessee Williams play.

*　　*　　*

William Carter's widow, Nina Pratt Carter (1863–1939) moved into the town of Plains with her five children, including Jimmy's father, James Earl. Taliaferro was twice tried on a charge of manslaughter, but on each occasion the jury failed to reach a verdict.

As a teenager, Jimmy was allowed to drive the family pickup truck into town for the weekend, and it was with his "pretty grandmother" Nina that he always stayed. She is buried next to her murdered husband in the same family plot as Uncle Alton's first wife, who bore the delightful name of Annie Laurie after the popular Scottish ballad. A bunch of blue hydrangea mark her grave in Plains Lebanon Cemetery.

Close by is the stone of Jimmy's father, who died of cancer in 1953. Dozens of footprints have been left by the tourists in the soft earth above his resting place.

The most elaborate of the monuments belongs to the Wise family. Their sanatorium became known for employing medical methods far in advance of its time. It was there that Lillian Gordy Carter took her nursing training and that Jimmy was born. Today the former sanatorium is a well-kept convalescent home for the aged of both races.

There is a segregated section of the cemetery for black dead of Plains. Although it is overgrown with weeds and shrubbery, there is a feeling that nature has taken over the spot, endowing it with a beauty and tranquility all its own.

*   *   *

John Carter, merchant, of Christ Church, Hampshire, England, was the father of the first of the Carter family to seek his fortune in America. Thomas Carter (1610–1669) paid his passage by signing up as an indentured servant, which was only one step above slavery. Often the black slaves were better fed, for an owner knew that they were his property forever or until he wished to sell them. When indentured servants served out their time, they were free to go where they pleased.

Thomas worked in Virginia where he had arrived at the age of twenty-five in 1635. Then, for some reason that is unknown, he went to the West Indies where he was captured by the Spaniards. After being imprisoned for twenty-one months, he escaped to his native England in a Dutch vessel.

Undaunted, Thomas Carter returned to Virginia prior to 1659, settling in Isle of Wight County, which had first been inhabited by the Warascoyak Indians who lived in a town on the Pagan River. This time, Thomas Carter, Jimmy Carter's ninth generation ancestor, was successful in the New World, importing indentured servants of his own from the Old.

His son, Thomas Carter, Jr. (1648–1710), joined Nathaniel Bacon's Rebellion, which involved battles with the Indians to enlarge the colonies. Since both the King of England and the Governor of Virginia opposed the rebellion, Carter could well have been executed.

In 1673, Thomas, Jr., married Magdalen Moore, the daughter of George Moore, Justice of the Court of Isle of Wight County, who gave the newlyweds four hundred acres of land. From that time on the American Carters were well established financially.

*　　*　　*

Like other landholders throughout the South, Jimmy's forebears were slave owners. Kindred Carter (1750–1800), due to a depression in North Carolina, moved his family into what was then an untamed region of western Georgia. Kindred's son, James, who married a Nellie Duckworth and lived to be 84, became a Baptist, the religious affiliation embraced by the Carters ever since.

*　　*　　*

By the summer of 1977, Jimmy Carter's Plains had come at times to resemble an amusement park.

The locals openly discussed the new breed of *carpetbagger*, who was moving in to profit from the small town's instant fame. Souvenir vendors were everywhere; For Sale signs sprung up like mushrooms.

Many longtime Plains residents thought their town had just become too crowded. Of course if 'Jimmy slept here,' that raised the price on a home. An enterprising Canadian was going to open a waxworks.

Two elaborate public conveniences, looking more like Japanese tea houses than anything else, had been built to accommodate the hundreds of visitors in search of Jimmy's roots. They looked sadly out of place against a backdrop of dignified Victorian-type homes festooned with their fair share of gingerbread carving.

Billy Carter had moved his family seventeen miles out of town for what he called "tourist protection." The sight-seeing buses even rumbled down the narrow dusty back-road that passed Miss Lillian's Pond House retreat.

Only Old Uncle Alton, shirt sleeves still rolled up, remained the same as ever. Nothing on earth could change that granite-like figure as he greeted all and sundry in his son's antique store.

_9_

WHEN the Carter clan arrived in New York City in July 1976 to attend the Democratic National Convention, New Yorkers got many opportunities to observe them at close range.

Rosalynn took Amy, who was dressed in bell bottom pants, to visit Central Park's Wonderland. Kicking off her sandals, Amy had a wonderful time swinging on ropes like a pint-sized Tarzan. Then she climbed into the cool lap of the Hans Christian Andersen statue. Here years before Fannie Hurst, the novelist, had read to neighborhood children, and Dame Margaret Rutherford, the veteran British actress and Oscar winner, had brought greetings from the Hans Christian Andersen Museum in Denmark. The moment was not lost on Amy, a bookworm herself and one of Andersen's most avid readers.

Later, sitting under the burning lights of Madison Square Garden, Rosalynn wore a bright red gown, as she watched Jimmy make his great announcement to the delegates: "My name is Jimmy Carter and I'm running for President . . ."

And it was Rosalynn, with a crimson floral lei hanging from her shoulders whom he lovingly embraced only moments after receiving the Democratic nomination.

Then, after Jimmy revealed his choice of running mate, Senator Fritz Mondale of Minnesota, a protégé of former Vice-President Hubert Humphrey, Carter and Mondale, with their wives Rosalynn and Joan, held hands together in a victory salute.

*   *   *

With victory half won, Jimmy and Rosalynn returned to Plains, where they were given an enthusiastic reception. Black and white residents joined together in a celebration that was memorable in once closely segregated Plains. Ida English provided a beautifully embroidered cloth for the head table.

There was, of course, little time for the Carters to rest or to cherish their remarkable accomplishment. The home stretch imposed harder campaigning than ever. "It's like a process of osmosis," said one of their friends, talking of Rosalynn at this unique period in her life. "Her drive and discipline are part of her own character."

"She has no time for comedy," said another. "She rarely wants to talk about books, movies, or sports. The only subject that animates her is Jimmy."

During this period, Rosalynn enjoyed her usual good health with the exception of her allergies, which were always with her. "I'm allergic to every allergy there is," she once said. Three times a week she needed her allergy shots.

When the press called her the "Steel Magnolia" and upset Jimmy, Rosalynn only laughed.

"I don't mind being called tough," she remarked. "I am strong, and I do have definite ideas and opinions. In the sense that tough means I can take a lot, stand up to a lot, it's a fair description."

The Carters and Mondales leave church in Plains, Ga., during the 1976 election campaign. *Wide World Photos*

*　　*　　*

Rosalynn was now considered so important a part of the Carter presidential organization that she was provided with two chartered Learjets. She traveled with an entourage of four or more Secret Service agents and three women from her own personal staff. Once off the plane, she led her motorcade to the endless rallies and personal appearances.

At none of the luncheons did she actually eat. That, in her opinion, would waste valuable campaigning time. Back on the plane she would enjoy her roast beef on rye, while the press corps in the other plane had their own donuts and sandwiches.

Before each public function, she was taken to a special "holding room" where she could rest, give short interviews, or make phone calls.

Although she had heard most of the questions put to her dozens of times before, Rosalynn was cordial and enthusiastic. Nothing seemed to ruffle her, even when persistently asked about her husband's controversial remarks on the subject of lust for *Playboy* magazine. For this question she had a standard reply, which she delivered in a firm quiet voice that seemed to say, "I dare you to contradict me."

"Jimmy," she would respond, "was explaining to a readership of 40 million what the Baptist religion, what Christianity means to him. The point he was making was 'Judge not lest ye be judged.' "

"Then of course," she would note with a hint of reproval, "his remarks need to be put in context."

*　　*　　*

Rosalynn was often compared with Betty Ford, who was actively campaigning for her own husband. Outspoken and extremely popular, Mrs. Ford was frequently referred to affectionately, by her Citizen's Band call, "First Mama."

While on a whirlwind one-day trip to most of New York's major cities, Rosalynn was asked about a possible rivalry with Mrs. Ford. Her answer was characteristic: "I've never felt any competition between me and Betty Ford. I'm running against Mr. Ford and his administration." She had personally enjoyed Mrs. Ford's visit to the Georgia Governor's Mansion.

Throughout New York State that same day, Rosalynn pressed her favorite causes: Jimmy, mental health, and senior citizens. Her statements of understanding and compassion for the elderly were impassioned: "I've become concerned about the elderly, for there's so much to be done. The elderly pay their taxes all their lives and get so little in return. My mother cried for two weeks when she had to retire from the post office in Plains. She said, 'I feel like I'm too old to do any good work.' Jimmy's mother is 78 and went to the Peace Corps when she was 68. Jimmy and I know the problems of the elderly first hand. So many people don't know what's available. There are all kinds of programs for the elderly, but the elderly don't know about them."

Speaking on mental health, Rosalynn indicated what she had in mind for the new administration: " I want Jimmy, if elected, to appoint a presidential commission on mental health, with volunteers working with me. This has not been done since John F. Kennedy's administration fifteen years ago."

Many of Rosalynn's remarks revealed her deep understanding of America's post-Watergate malaise: "Throughout the whole country, people are looking for stability. If you can develop a caring society, then people are looking for that opportunity. If the people know the problems and

86

if they trust the government, they will help solve those problems. People are afraid to hope again."

When asked about her stand on the Equal Rights Amendment (ERA), Rosalynn went on record as saying, "I support ERA. It means equal rights for women and equal pay for an equal job done."

Of all women, Rosalynn should know. She had taken an equal role with Jimmy in making their peanut business a success, to say nothing of her own untiring role in Jimmy's fight for the Presidency.

*   *   *

Towards the campaign's end, husband and wife made a joint appearance in Virginia. There Rosalynn stood up to give the speech he had never heard. It proved rather an emotional moment for Jimmy; his eyes were damp with tears.

Looking first into the sea of strange faces in the audience and then at the dear familiar one, she began:

"I've known him all my life. I think his background is important, the fact that he's a farmer, that he's worked for a living. I worked . . ." Jimmy looked up and swallowed hard.

"The children worked," she went on. "I kept the books. We worked hard. We scrimped and saved to make the business a success."

She paused. One could have heard a pin drop. "When he was Governor, he abolished 278 of 300 agencies. He got the phone company to check how much waste there was, and he saved $800 just on the phone bills. Jimmy Carter knows human beings in this country . . . and Jimmy has never had any hint of scandal in his business or personal life."

As she finished, Jimmy kissed and held her so tightly she was lifted clear off the ground. It was a rare moment as the youthful grandparents publicly embraced. They struck a blow for the wholesome kind of family life they both loved best.

"That's beautiful . . . beautiful." Jimmy told her over and over. Then putting his arm protectively around her waist, he asked: "How many of you would like to have Rosalynn as First Lady?"

As the audience roared their approval, Jimmy smiled.

"*And so would I*," he said.

Rosalynn campaigning with son Jeff and his wife and Jimmy at the Palace of Fine Arts Theater in San Francisco just after Carter's second debate with President Ford. *Wide World Photos*

_10_

CASUALLY dressed in checkered slacks and warm topcoat, Rosalynn strolled beside Jimmy to the polling place in Plains to vote for her favorite candidate. "I have done all I could," she said.

The thousands of miles she had covered alone had been unique in the long history of prospective First Ladies. Now it was almost over; a few more hours and she would know if all the work had been in vain.

She had cooked scrambled eggs for breakfast, made sure that Jimmy was wearing a warm cardigan for it was a chilly morning, and then, hand in hand with Jimmy, she headed toward their destiny. A smell of bonfire ash floated over the rooftops. The calm of Plains that morning contrasted with the tumultuous welcome given them both only a few mornings before when, riding in an open limousine, they visited New York City's bustling Garment District.

*   *   *

After casting their votes, they left with an excited Amy for Atlanta to anxiously await the first returns. It was a long prayerful day for Rosalynn, a time for thinking and for

91

going over the past. A time for reflecting on how wonderfully varied her life had been. Four fine children, one even born in exotic Hawaii. A devoted husband who still liked to call her "my bride." She thought of her schooldays and Miss Julia, of her loving father who died years before his time, and of her mother who was still respected as an example of quiet kindliness in Plains. The years of peanut farming, of working long hours at the accounts in the warehouse, had all meant a great deal to her. She had been First Lady of Georgia, and now, perhaps before morning, she would be the wife of the President-elect of the United States. Rosalynn felt that she had truly been blessed among women.

*   *   *

During the early hours of the following day, Jimmy Carter was declared the victor over the incumbent President Gerald R. Ford. At 3:28 A.M., his total electoral vote reached 272, two more than the 270 needed to win the election.

Carrying a sleeping Amy in his arms, President-elect Carter, with the new First Lady, headed home to Plains to share the victory with family and friends. Plains responded nobly; the entire town, young and old, came out to greet them.

Fires blazed merrily in old oil drums to warm those who had loyally waited out the long night. Many were wrapped in warm blankets. It was a rare, emotional moment when Jimmy and Rosalynn faced the crowd from the platform of the old railroad depot and looked out towards the silhouette that was their native Plains. Miss Julia Coleman had been right all those years before when she had said in her clear, firm voice, daring anybody to contradict her: "A boy, however humble his origins, can still grow up and become President of his country."

Jimmy's throat seemed tight with emotion, and even Rosalynn, usually so self-controlled, dabbed at her tearing eyes. "I came all the way through . . . I told you I didn't intend to lose," Jimmy began, with what voice he had left from the long struggle for the Presidency.

Then he turned to his Rosalynn, his voice choking as he embraced her. Quickly regaining his composure, he continued, "It was a long night, but I guarantee you, it's going to be worth it to all of us."

Tears glistened on Miss Lillian's wrinkled cheeks as she nodded in approval. Miss Allie glowed with quiet pride. Nor did Jimmy forget the defeated President Ford in his own hour of victory, calling him "a good and decent man."

*   *   *

From Albany, Georgia, on November 6, Rosalynn and Jimmy boarded the special jet provided them by President Ford. They flew to St. Simon's Island, a settlement famous from Colonial times whose history has been told in the best-selling novels of local author, Eugenia Price.

St. Simon's, with its giant lighthouse presiding over a long pier where the local residents stroll and fish on warm evenings, provided just the sort of relaxing atmosphere that Jimmy and Rosalynn needed in which to unwind. They both arrived casually dressed and, as usual, toting their own luggage. The President-elect's favorite well-worn pair of boots, which he carried in his hand, drew plenty of smiles. He said that he planned to walk, work, fish, and sleep while a guest on secluded Musgrove Plantation.

"This is what I've been waiting for," Jimmy told Rosalynn as they admired the plane's presidential seal. This was *Air Force One*, the same historic plane that had carried President Kennedy's body home to the White House after the assassination in Dallas. Years later, President and Mrs. Richard M. Nixon flew in it for their trip to China.

While aboard, the Carters examined the photographs on the cabin walls. A floodlit White House, President Ford greeting Pele, the soccer star, and a smiling closeup of Betty Ford, whose First Lady role Rosalynn would soon take over.

The next morning, Jimmy and Caron, Chip's wife, attended morning services at Christ Episcopal Church, a white, steepled building standing in an ancient graveyard beneath oaks festooned with Spanish moss. Later in the day, while Rosalynn enjoyed the company of their first grandson, Jason, who was then a toddler and into everything, Jimmy played pool and Ping-Pong with sons Jack and Chip. He later took Amy for a swim that didn't last long—the water was too chilly.

*   *   *

When he wasn't working on that hefty box of transition papers he had personally carried off the plane, Jimmy walked with Rosalynn, hand in hand, on long strolls through the secluded grounds and along the shore.

The photographs that emerged from this postelection retreat at St. Simon's included one picture of a solitary Jimmy framed with a natural background of marsh reeds and water. It evoked the loneliness of the presidency and bore an uncanny similarity to a well-remembered photograph of President John F. Kennedy taking a solitary walk on the wet sands of Hyannisport. That earlier picture came out of a period when the whole country had undergone a spiritual rebirth, inspired by the youthful Jack and Jackie Kennedy with all their splendid dreams of Camelot.

Now it was Jimmy and Rosalynn, two ordinary Americans from a small Southern town whose entire population was less than 700. With Watergate finally behind them, the people's hope and trust centered on the good looking couple from Plains.

*   *   *

While her husband was involved with two days of important transitional talks in Washington, including a meeting with outgoing President Ford, Rosalynn was equally busy greeting old friends who had worked so hard to elect her husband. She also spent many hours conferring with her newly appointed press secretary, Mrs. Mary Finch Hoyt.

Accompanied by Mrs. Hoyt and Chip, Rosalynn visited Stevens Elementary School, built 108 years before for the children of ex-slaves. A few days later it was officially announced that following her father's Inauguration on January 20, Amy would be attending the integrated school. This meant that Amy would be making history of her own. She would be the first presidential child to attend a public school since Theodore Roosevelt's son, Quentin, in 1906.

Both Jimmy and Rosalynn had declared many times that if the former won the election they would be sending Amy to an integrated public school, just as they had in Plains. Jimmy put their views bluntly when he said, "People ask where I stand on the issues. I stand with my daughter. She's not in some all-white suburban school or some private school with a black or two in it for show. She's in a class that's more than half black, and she doesn't keep count, I'll tell you."

The new school had 213 students of which about sixty percent were black. Children from Washington's foreign diplomatic corps and their employees made up some thirty percent of the enrollment. Rosalynn said in her formal announcement that Amy had already received letters from some of her future schoolmates and her fourth grade teacher.

"She is particularly eager to attend class with so many children from foreign nations," said Rosalynn. "I have visited Thaddeus Stevens School, which is located near the White House, and was very pleased with the quality of the school, the attitude of the staff, teachers, and the friendliness of the students. We understand that this is the school that Amy will be assigned to by the school officials. No special security problems have been found to exist.

"All of us want to be a constructive part of the Washington community, and as parents, Jimmy and I are grateful to our future neighbors who have already done so much to make us feel welcome."

Thaddeus Stevens School, an old, red brick building stands in the middle of what is commonly called "Restaurant Row." Smells of exotic cooking often greeted the children entering and leaving the school.

*   *   *

Home in Plains for Thanksgiving, Rosalynn Carter, like other American housewives, prepared the festive dinner herself with some help from Amy. The meal included traditional roast turkey, cornbread dressing, brussels sprouts served with brown butter, green beans from the garden, homemade hot rolls, and ambrosia, a citrus fruit dish decorated with coconut topping. There were, in addition, two of Rosalynn's specialties: grapefruit and avocado salad, and Jimmy's favorite cheese-ring dessert garnished with rich strawberry preserves.

Sitting down for Thanksgiving dinner were Miss Allie and Miss Lillian, Jack, Chip, Jeff, and their wives, Amy, and little Jason.

*   *   *

In his first Thanksgiving message, Jimmy spoke from the heart: "My thoughts always return to my wife, Rosalynn, my own family, and the people of my community who worked so hard to help me, who shared the bad times as well as the good, and who I always knew would be my friends and my family whether I won or lost."

Then he gave special thanks for: "An America on the move again, united, its wounds healed, its head high, moving into its third century with confidence, competence, and compassion, an America that lives up to the majesty of its Constitution and the simple decency of its people.

"For what our country is, for what it can be, but most of all for the opportunity each of us has to make our vision of America a reality—*I am thankful.*"

_11_

WELCOME BARBARA WALTERS

The Best Western Motel in Americus, ten miles from Plains, was awaiting the arrival of ABC's million dollar personality who was coming to interview Jimmy and Rosalynn inside their own home. On the other side of the motel sign were the words:

WELCOME BABS ELIOT

the name that Miss Walters had used in the days she had yearnings to become a Rockette in New York's Radio City. During the night, a prankster had changed the first sign to

WELCOME BARBARA WAWA

but it was discovered in time and corrected.

By now the motel staff were getting used to the arrival of celebrities, although some admitted to feeling somewhat awed at the prospect of meeting Miss Walters. They were to find her a pleasant and considerate guest, and the television interview with Jimmy and Rosalynn inside their unpretentious ranch-house home turned out to be one of Barbara's best.

She interviewed the Carters as they sat on a comfortable sofa in their den. In every room, the cameras picked up pictures of Amy at various ages while there was a slide rule picture showing her growth in feet and inches. The story of Amy's 'miracle' birth was retold. Then Rosalynn confessed that Jimmy actually found time during their busy campaign days to pen her a thirtieth wedding anniversary letter.

Jimmy in turn denied the stories that Rosalynn was "tough and ambitious." "She's a very soft and reticent person. There's nothing harsh or insensitive about her at all," he said as he held her hand.

With a smile, he insisted they would take their blue jeans to the White House, but promised not to wear them to greet the French Ambassador. Rosalynn said she would ship no furniture from home to Washington with the exception of her precious sewing machine. She commented that she would like to have a square dance in the White House. "We had one at the Governor's Mansion when Jimmy was Governor," she said as her face lit up with that little girl smile at the memory.

Then Barbara asked Jimmy the fifty dollar question: "Do you sleep in a double bed or twin beds?"

"Well," said Jimmy looking at Rosalynn for moral support, "sometimes we sleep in a single bed by ourself, but it's much more comfortable in a double bed."

* * *

Jimmy and Rosalynn were out voting again, this time to elect the new mayor of Plains. Jimmy's irrepressible younger brother Billy was running to unseat the incumbent mayor and Plains only barber, A. L. (Loren) Blanton. It rained hard all day, which must have been a bad omen for Billy, who lost 90–71.

Ironically, Billy Carter declared that his reason for running was to stop his home town from becoming a tourist trap.

He promised that, if elected, his first act would be to order the removal of a plastic Christmas tree donated to Plains by a North Carolina man. "There is a wealth of real trees around here," grumbled Billy, "and Plains ought to have a real Christmas tree."

* * *

Rosalynn, who has always had a special love for Mexico, was invited to attend the Inaugural in Mexico City of the President of Mexico, José López Portillo. She attended as the personal friend of President Portillo's wife.

She was perfectly at ease in what might have been a dress rehearsal for when she would officially represent Jimmy on missions to Latin countries. Her large, dangling earrings were admired by the Mexican ladies. Secretary of State Henry Kissinger was especially courteous, helping Rosalynn with points of protocol, and Jack Ford, handsome son of President Ford, was representing his father at the ceremonies. He greeted Rosalynn with a broad smile.

* * *

In the weeks before the Inaugural, the President-elect's staff announced that the name "Jimmy Carter" instead of "James Earl Carter" would appear on the official 1977 Inaugural Medal.

There was also news of the First Lady's Inaugural Ball gown. Plains matrons such as Ida English had been confident that Rosalynn Carter would make her own on that famous sewing machine she loved so much. It would have been quite in character. Instead, her new staff announced that she would wear the same blue chiffon gown she had worn at the Georgia Governor's Inaugural Ball several years previously. She was attached to it and so was Jimmy. For sentimental reasons, Rosalynn would wear it again and so ensure its posterity in the First Lady Gowns Collection at the Smithsonian Institution. Many hopeful dress designers were outraged, but Rosalynn, as always, stood firm.

*   *   *

As Christmas Day 1976 grew closer, Miss Lillian, then 78, who usually prepared the family breakfast with grits and homemade sausage conveniently provided by Carter-raised hogs, had to be admitted to the Americus-Sumter County Hospital for special heat treatments. They were necessary to ease a painful arthritic condition.

As in other years, Jimmy's immediate family searched the nearby woods for a cedar tree that, according to Ann Anderson, Rosalynn's Deputy Press Secretary, was "not a big beautiful tree, but a scraggly one that is not doing so well." It was decorated by Amy and Rosalynn with old familiar ornaments that had been made by the Carter children when they were small and that were carefully treasured by their mother.

On Christmas morning Amy was wide awake at five, promptly waking her parents too. Santa Claus had brought her a large and fully furnished Cape Cod doll house, which she decided then and there would go with her to the White House. She also received her own telephone, which was something of a novelty as it was the first pushbutton phone in Plains.

Jimmy gave Rosalynn a nightgown and robe. Her gift to him created the most interest in the press. It was an oil painting done in blues, browns, and golds and entitled *The Brown Farm*. A 39-year-old local Georgian, Butler Brown, was the artist; he is Jimmy's favorite. Rosalynn had bought him a smaller Butler Brown canvas some years before. *The Brown Farm*, destined to be hung in the White House, portrayed an old home with two well-used barns in the background.

Brown, who grew up in the small town of Hawkinsville, Georgia, came to Jimmy's notice when, as Governor, he visited the artist's one-man show at a Macon art gallery. Jimmy immediately felt a great affinity for the rustic subjects that were exhibited, telling a delighted Brown that he could "relate" to his work. Ann Tutt, the gallery owner, then hung one of Butler Brown's farm scenes in Jimmy's Atlanta office. When visiting Secretary of State Henry Kissinger saw it, he exclaimed, "I see you have a Wyeth."

Jimmy laughed. "No, a Butler Brown," he said.

Later Jimmy sent Brown a photograph of himself with Kissinger admiring the painting, underneath of which he wrote: "To my friend Butler Brown. Kissinger shares my admiration for your work."

Butler Brown's love of the red land Rosalynn and Jimmy are so fond of was himself born in Central Georgia. His first memories are of watching his father weigh cotton and seeing a venerable pecan tree be uprooted by a tornado and thrown over his mother's washtub.

*   *   *

That year the family exchanged gifts at Miss Lillian's hospital bedside. Jimmy and Rosalynn gave her an album of photographs showing her four children from babyhood upwards. It was the best tonic that Miss Lillian could have had. Her chief complaint was "I'm getting old so fast."

On leaving the hospital, Jimmy grinned boyishly and said, "It's a good Christmas. The only difference is that, instead of being at mother's house, we were at the hospital."

Then, carrying a large bag of presents, Jimmy drove with Rosalynn, Amy, Chip, and Caron to an Americus motel for breakfast. There they were joined by Billy, his amiable wife Sybil, and their baby son, Earl.

Later Amy read aloud the story of the First Christmas from her Bible while the family sat around their Christmas tree, festooned as it was with so many memories of other happy holidays.

Miss Allie presided over a turkey dinner in her own home. Jimmy was treated to what Rosalynn calls his "all-time favorite," Japanese fruit cake, made in four generous layers filled with raisins, lemon rind, crushed pineapple filling, coconut, and spice.

_13_

"IT is a very distinct honor for our church to have had one of our own become the leader of this nation. We enter in a covenant, Jimmy and Rosalynn, to pray for you and the tremendous responsibility that you have as our President and First Lady."

Rosalynn and Jimmy listened appreciatively as the Reverend Bruce Edwards bade them Godspeed and farewell at their last Sunday morning service before leaving Plains for the Presidential Inauguration in Washington.

Before the service Jimmy had attended the men's Bible class sitting behind members of the Atlanta Braves baseball team. The day before they had played a softball game against the Plains All Stars led by brother Billy.

"All Christians and especially those labeled Baptists will share in the spotlight that shines on Jimmy and Rosalynn," Dean Clarence Dodson, the Bible class teacher, told them.

Then the President-elect was presented with a silver Bible marker, and it was his turn to speak: "You know how much this class has meant to me. I hope that as I undertake to serve this nation, I can so order my convictions and ideals so that this class will be proud of everything I do and that my performance will be measured in God's eyes to the satisfaction of His Kingdom."

Standing in the churchyard with Amy somewhat lost beneath the high cape collar of her new top-coat, Jimmy said that it had been an "emotional farewell . . . especially with the women. Many of them were my teachers."

*   *   *

The next morning, after Rosalynn has prepared scrambled eggs for their breakfast and fried thick slices of rich Georgia ham, they were on hand to bid good-bye and Godspeed to friends and neighbors who were traveling on a special eighteen-car Amtrak train, dubbed the Peanut Special, for the Inauguration ceremonies in Washington. It was the first passenger train to leave Plains in twenty years. With the 10° weather, Deacon Turner's hardware store had sold out of longjohns.

There was actually snow and ice festooning the pines, the first in octogenarian Uncle Alton Carter's memory. Uncle Alton had declined going to Washington himself for all the celebrating. "I'm too old," he insisted. Instead he stayed home and "kept the store."

Looking at the snow, Sam Simpson, a Barnesville, Georgia, grocer, who was wearing an appropriate peanut lei offset by two peanut bracelets, observed with a touch of irony, "My granddaddy told me that hell would freeze over before we'd have a Southerner as President. Well, I just heard say that Washington is frozen!"

*   *   *

"Behave yourself now, and if you get in trouble, don't call me," Jimmy kidded Virginia Williams, a former high school classmate.

Maxine Reese, the outgoing and pleasant woman who had managed the Carter Campaign Headquarters in Plains, had hired the train and made all the arrangements for the memorable trip.

Standing on the old depot platform with his arm cradling Rosalynn, the future President and his First Lady waved good-bye. The Peanut Special was on its way.

*   *   *

Jimmy had personally helped to load the small rented van that would take Amy's Cape Cod doll house, Rosalynn's sewing machine, and other personal belongings to the White House. Driven by one of Billy Carter's warehouse men, the van had to return shortly after leaving when Amy's bicycle was found to have been forgotten.

Just before noon, the man who the next day would be President of the United States turned off the water and electricity and lowered the thermostat of the house that Rosalynn and he had built as their final home. Now the house was handed over to a caretaker and the Secret Service as Mr. and Mrs. Jimmy Carter and daughter Amy flew off to their exciting new life in Washington. With them was Misty Malarky Ying Yang, Amy's Siamese cat.

Amy, who had already visited the White House once, when she had fallen in love with the beautiful so-called Queen's Bedroom, was worried over the safety of her treasured doll's house.

Upon arrival in Washington, Amy was reunited with her former nurse, Mary Fitzpatrick, who had been granted a special furlough from prison to care for her during the festivities.

Mary, who had kept all the other inmates awake with excitement on election night, had her traveling expenses paid by Atlanta's Junior League. Fellow prisoners contributed the velvet for a formal evening gown. A jubilant and smiling Mary arrived in Washington wearing a large orchid corsage pinned to her mock leopard-skin lapel.

*   *   *

That evening Rosalynn, looking resplendent in a black blouse offset by a long, red skirt, entered the presidential box at the Kennedy Center accompanied by Jimmy in a black tuxedo and Amy in a crimson sweater. Actress Shirley MacLaine appropriately opened the 1977 New Spirit Inaugural Concert with a new version of Cy Coleman's "It's Not Where You Start." She smiled knowingly at Jimmy and Rosalynn as she reached the final lines . . .

> It's where you finish
> And you've finished on
> Top.

*   *   *

Other highlights included Republican John Wayne, King of the Westerns, drawling into the microphone, "I am considered a member of the Opposition—The Loyal Opposition. Accent the *loyal*. I'd have it no other way."

Aretha Franklin had everyone, Jimmy, Rosalynn, and Amy included, clapping in old time rhythm as she sang. The most poignant moment came as Leonard Bernstein conducted the National Symphony Orchestra, presenting his own composition, "If Ever Man Were Loved by Wife." *He dedicated it to Rosalynn.*

Later at a postconcert dinner, veteran actress, Bette Davis, a dedicated Democrat, with a hand over her heart exclaimed, "Oh, I want so much to shake his hand." When Jimmy gave her a big hug the great Davis was left smiling.

*   *   *

With a blue-coated Rosalynn holding the Carter family Bible upon which her husband rested a hand, the moment for which she had worked so long had at last arrived. As she looked proudly into Jimmy's eyes, Chief Justice Warren Burger solemnly asked: "Are you ready to take the Oath of Office?"

It was 12:30 P.M. A hush fell over the great gathering in front of the Capitol. The Bible used at the Inauguration of George Washington lay open at the Book of Micah.

After Jimmy had been sworn in as the thirty-ninth President of the United States, the Chief Justice offered his personal congratulations. Then the Marine Band played "Hail to the Chief," followed by a twenty-one-gun salute.

Jimmy Carter from Plains, Georgia, had finally reached the White House. He was the first Southern President since the War between the States. There were wet eyes in the crowd when an all black choir dramatically sang "The Battle Hymn of the Republic."

The Inaugural Address was of a more personal nature than those of many previous presidents. Jimmy thanked outgoing Gerald Ford "for all he has done to heal our land." Then he mentioned Rosalynn and his beloved teacher, dead three years, but surely there in spirit: "As my high school teacher, Miss Julia Coleman, used to say, 'We must adjust to changing times and still hold to unchanging principles.'"

Jimmy quoted his favorite Old Testament prophet saying, "I have just taken the oath of office on the Bible my Mother gave me a few years ago, opened to a timeless admonition from the ancient prophet Micah:

'He hath showed thee, O man, what is good; and what doth the Lord require of thee, but to do justly, and to love mercy, and to walk humbly with thy God.'

"I join in the hope that when my time as your President has ended, people might say this about our nation: That we had remembered the words of Micah and renewed our search for humility, mercy, and justice."

Jimmy Carter takes the oath of office as the 39th President of the United States at the Capitol as Rosalynn holds the Bible. *Wide World Photos*

Then after lunch, on that sunny but subfreezing day, President and Mrs. Jimmy Carter, with members of their family, treated not only the crowds estimated at 250,000 people, but the entire nation via television to a sight they had never seen before—a new President walking down Pennsylvania Avenue, a distance of a mile and a half. With Jimmy and Rosalynn hand in hand leading the way, and a fur booted Amy in the middle, it was something to be cherished and remembered. For the Carters themselves it was a symbolic walk; they had both stressed so often that Jimmy, if elected to executive office, would always stay close to the people. It was truly a family occasion, with little Jason riding on his father Jack's broad shoulder and his Aunt Amy playing "Step on a Crack, Break Your Mother's Back."

As they reached the doorway of their new home, the White House, Jimmy asked: "Where Do I live?" Chief Usher Rex Scouten escorted the First Family to their new quarters.

Later, Jimmy and Rosalynn, a little awed by the great sense of history, walked slowly through the Executive Mansion. Said Jimmy afterwards, "I thought I'd look around. I never have seen it."

*   *   *

For the two-hour-long Inaugural Parade, the Carters and Mondales watched from a solar-heated reviewing stand designed to call attention to Jimmy's environmental interests.

That evening with the new President wearing a tuxedo and Rosalynn her favorite blue chiffon, they made a tour of the five Inauguration parties held in various parts of the city. Amy, looking very grown up in her own long gown, was on hand for two of them.

At the Hotel Mayflower, the President and First Lady danced together to the strains of "The Last Waltz." Then, kissing her tenderly, he jokingly asked some of the guests, "Don't you like my wife's old dress?"

President and Mrs. Carter were back at the White House by 12:30 A.M., much earlier than expected. They were both tired out. Rosalynn called it "a perfect day."

*　　*　　*

The next day the Carters were busy receiving guests at special White House receptions. About a thousand attended the first of these gatherings, which were designed to thank people who had entertained a member of the Carter family overnight during the campaign. "These are my kinsfolk," Jimmy said.

At another reception were members of the Peanut Special, whose visit to Washington had turned into an occasion memorable as much for its discomfort as anything else. They had arrived to find that their hotel's heating system had broken down. There was also a shortage of blankets in the heatless rooms. The next day their scheduled transportation to the Inaugural ceremony failed to arrive, so that after traveling all the way from Plains, some of them actually missed it.

The White House reception for the travellers from Plains was genuine and "down home" in feeling. There were hugs and kisses from Jimmy, Rosalynn, and Miss Lillian. As Bill English told me later in Plains, "Everyone should take just one trip like it in a lifetime—but only one."

*　　*　　*

Before Mary Fitzpatrick returned to jail, Rosalynn asked her, "How would you like to work in this big old place?"

112

A few days later Mary was.

President and Mrs. Carter personally requested that she be given a preparole reprieve from her life sentence. As she arrived back in Washington to resume her duties as Amy's nurse, this time for good, Mary's comment was, "I think it's unbelievable this is happening to me."

Said Rosalynn, "Mary is a good person. I trust her completely."

_14_

WITH one of the worst Washington winters on record and Jimmy's setting the White House thermostat at 60° to conserve energy, Rosalynn complained that the only place she could find to keep warm was the kitchen. The Carter family's first days in the Executive Mansion were spent wearing warm cardigans and sweaters.

It was not until the Kennedy administration that a special kitchen and dining room were installed in the First Family's living quarters. They have been a joy to every presidential family since. On those bitterly cold days, Rosalynn silently blessed Jackie Kennedy Onassis for her thoughtfulness.

From the moment that Rosalynn and Jimmy wake in their double bed at 6:00 A.M. until he turns out the bedside light at midnight, her day is as busy as his. She likes to eat breakfast with Amy who, like so many small girls, enjoys sharing her school secrets with her mother. Blue jeans and blouses are still hemmed on the famous sewing machine, just as they were in Plains. Rosalynn, from the beginning, has always found time to do these small tasks for her child.

When Amy began to take violin lessons, Rosalynn decided to join her. Jimmy remarked that he would soon have his own all-woman orchestra.

Amy also took up photography, printing and developing her own work. She always gave her mother the first look at her efforts, which turned out to be quite good.

Early in February, Mary Fitzpatrick, at the personal request of President and Mrs. Carter, won a preparole reprieve and arrived to continue her duties as Amy's nurse. There was no more delighted child in the whole of Washington that morning than the one in the White House. The vibrant picture of Mary embracing Amy—literally sweeping the little girl off her feet—softened many doubting hearts concerning loyal Mary's fitness for the role.

*   *   *

Although she was twelve minutes late, Amy's first day at Thaddeus Stevens Elementary School was a happy one. Wearing blue jeans, a blue raincoat, a white and red Snoopy sweater that bore the words "Keep 'Em Flying," and a bright wool hat, she arrived on the hand of her mother. She was put in the fourth grade.

Crowds lined the office windows opposite for a glimpse of Amy and the new First Lady. The words "Welcome Amy Carter" hung on the classroom door. "Good morning, Mrs. Carter," the class said in unison. Amy greeted her teacher, Verona Meeder, and Rosalynn left, but two secret service agents sat outside the classroom door as Amy did her lessons.

"She's real smart because she writes real neat," praised Maurice Brown, one of her new classmates. Under a doodle-bird mobile that hung in the center of the room, Amy felt very much at home reading *Paul Revere's Ride*, practicing handwriting, and learning the mysteries of yards, inches, and meters. She ate her hot school lunch, costing $1.75 a week, with her new friends.

Mrs. Meeder said afterwards that Amy was "very unaffected, very natural, very independent. She just fit in beautifully."

Amy was also the delighted recipient of a special present from her new teacher, a large, fluffy, black and white mongrel puppy, who was immediately christened "Grits." Misty Malarky Ying Yang, the Siamese cat, accepted the new White House arrival with some misgivings, but allowed him to spend the night on the pink rug in Amy's bedroom. The next morning Grits was moved to the kennel to await Amy's return from her second day at school. "I think Amy's really going to like her new school," said Rosalynn.

Amy soon made special friends and before long was bringing them home. It wasn't everybody who had a private screening room for such delights as Walt Disney's *Freaky Friday* and, later, Tatum O'Neal's *National Velvet*, Amy's favorite movie.

Claudia Sanchez, the daughter of a Chilean Embassy cook, was invited to stay overnight. It was Claudia who had shown Amy where to hang her coat on her first day at school. Like most nine-year-olds they adored mysteries and were intrigued by the White House's secret passage. Then there was the Lincoln ghost. Both children were allowed to spend the night in the huge Lincoln bed, while Mary Fitzpatrick slept on a pallet on the floor.

"Of course," says Rosalynn with a smile, "they heard the ghost."

*   *   *

Although Rosalynn and Jimmy were commended by many for sending their child to a racially integrated public school, they soon realised that the American people were still going to treat her as a celebrity. Amy for the next four years would have to endure almost royalty status. Mrs. Lydia Williams, principal of the Thaddeus Stevens Elementary School, admitted that this was the first time in the school's 108-year-history that it had a waiting list for prospective students.

*   *   *

On February 6, dressed all in white, Amy was baptized by total immersion in Washington's First Baptist Church. From a sixth-row pew Jimmy, Chip, Caron, and Mary Fitzpatrick watched as the pastor, Dr. Charles A. Trentham, performed the ceremony: "Amy Carter, upon your confession of faith in Christ as your Saviour and Lord, and in obedience to His commandments, I baptize you my sister, in the name of the father and of the Son and of the Holy Spirit."

Rosalynn, who had been waiting behind the pool, then took Amy into a waiting room to change into dry clothes. Baptism in the Carters' faith is not performed shortly after birth as in many other denominations, but when the child reaches "the age of accountability."

One day during those first months in Washington, Amy decided that she would like a tree house of her own in a White House thicket. Her father volunteered to be architect. As a child in Plains, the President had his own tree house of which his memories were both pleasant and painful. When his father called him down one day, he at first refused to obey, and when he did, he found a peach switch waiting for him.

White House carpenters used left over lumber for Amy's treehouse, and they built it among the branches of a sturdy old Atlas cedar in such a way that it was not actually nailed to the tree.

117

Rosalynn and Jimmy Carter hold hands as they leave Sunday church services. *Wide World Photos*

With her special tree-house view of the Jefferson Memorial and Washington Monument, Amy enjoys reading quietly among the branches on warm days. When Aunt Amy took twenty-month-old nephew, Jason, to visit her new hideaway, she knelt in the four-by-five-foot platform to answer a few questions. Asked by white House reporters if her father ever visited her there, she replied, "Sometimes. He climbed up here once."

*   *   *

Rosalynn and Jimmy both enjoyed exercizing the traditional presidential prerogative of choosing which paintings to hang in the family quarters. "It was like Christmas," said Rosalynn. "Here were all these great paintings, and you could pick any you wanted."

Clement E. Conger, the White House curator, said that the Carters asked for something "bright and sunny and cheerful—like American Impressionists." "Dismissal of School on an October Afternoon" by Henry Inman was chosen for Amy's bedroom. For their own, the Carters requested "The House on the Marne" by Cézanne. They chose "The Crimson Rambler" by Philip L. Hale for the West Sitting Hall, where they like to relax after supper. This canvas reminded Rosalynn of her "grandmother's place."

In February, Jimmy asked Conger to write him up a history of all the works of art in the Oval Office. These included Frederic Remington's famed bronze *Bronco Buster* and the only known replica painting of George Washington's portrait by Charles Willson Peale, which is valued at from $400,000 to $600,000. A painting of a stalk of celery, a teapot, and a tomato by spare-time artist Rosalynn Carter still hangs in the kitchen in Plains.

*   *   *

One consolation of moving into the White House was the renewed togetherness that Rosalynn was able to enjoy with Jimmy and Amy after her many months on the campaign trail. She and Jimmy began having lunches together frequently, with the food brought in on trays. Supper is always a family affair when they all hold hands and say grace together. If Jimmy works overtime in the Oval Office, Amy is sent to fetch him. Her father is noted for his punctuality, so this does not happen often. Eli Young, a tall waiter in neat tuxedo, serves the meal for which a typical down-home main course would be pork chops, mashed potatoes, and broccoli.

Rosalynn also found time to baby-sit for Caron and Chip's newborn son, James Earl Carter IV. While she played tennis with Jimmy, the baby slept happily in his carriage by the court.

*   *   *

With Amy asleep, Rosalynn and Jimmy enjoy their Bible reading together. Many of their predecessors in the White House are known to have drawn closer to their religion after taking office. Perhaps this has been true of the Carters as well, and there was one change in their pattern of worship that Jimmy once commented on: "I changed from reading a chapter in the Bible every night in English to reading one in Spanish. Early this spring, my wife began to take Spanish lessons. So now one night she reads a chapter, and the next night I read a chapter . . .

"This is something that has meant a lot to us both. I am now going through the New Testament for the third time. And when we get through this time, we are going to start through the Old Testament.

"We do this the last thing every night, and we never miss. It is something that we kind of look forward to now."

Rosalynn with grandson James Earl Carter IV in the family quarters in the White House. *Wide World Photos*

Rosalynn during an interview at the White House.

_15_

ROSALYNN and Jimmy soon discovered that the one place they could relax in peace away from press and public was Camp David, the presidential retreat located on Catoctin Mountain. There they could enjoy rare moments of privacy that they could no longer find on visits home to Plains. Said Jimmy of the quiet and seclusion at Camp David, "We need to keep it that way."

Residents of neighboring Thurmont, Maryland, were delighted when Jimmy retained the name "Camp David," so christened by President Eisenhower in honor of his grandson, David. Formerly it had been dubbed "Shangri-la" by President Franklin D. Roosevelt, whose many visits there were spent in plotting World War II strategy, entertaining foreign officials, and attending to his beloved stamp collection.

Rosalynn and Jimmy enjoy the tennis courts and the miles of trails that weave the woods adjoining the four-bedroom main residence, Aspen Lodge, and the ten fireplace-equipped guest cabins. High barbed-wire fences surround Camp David, and there are guard towers and armed Marine patrols. The site also has underground bomb shelters and the latest communications equipment to keep President Carter in touch with the rest of the world.

Camp David was to achieve international importance as the site of the Sadat-Begin talks in 1978 with President Carter working as mediator. At that time Rosalynn proved the perfect hostess, quiet and efficient, dividing her time between Camp David and Washington. It was also her job to make Mrs. Begin feel at home. President Sadat did not bring his wife to America on that occasion.

*   *   *

Although Camp David came under the scrutiny of those members of Jimmy's staff assigned to make sure that his would be a "no frills" administration, the mountain retreat survived the onslaught. Other, less justifiable amenities did not. Many White House officials, for example, lost their color televisions, which had been valued as status symbols during previous administrations.

Jimmy and Rosalynn, who enjoyed having their two younger sons with their wives, one grandchild, a parakeet living with them in the White House, responded quickly when some of the taxpayers began to question the expense of housing so much of the Carter family. On a radio talk show in the spring of 1977, Jimmy explained, "I want the American people to know that we are not mooching off the American taxpayer. All the personal expenses of our family are paid for out of my own pocket or the pockets of my children."

The Carters had become the first extended presidential family to live in the White House since Franklin and Eleanor Roosevelt's daughter Anna went home to her parents and lived there with her two children, Sistie and Buzzie, following her divorce from her first husband, Curtis B. Dall. Each month, Rex Scouten, the chief usher, bills the Carters (Rosalynn is given the bill) for clothing, for food eaten at family meals, and for private entertainment costs and in-patient medical care. When Chip and Caron's baby was born in the National Naval Medical Center, Bethesda, Maryland, they paid the bill themselves.

In Plains, Chip and Caron had lived in "the second trailer down from the post office." It was buff colored and became such a tourist attraction that it has now been removed from its site. On moving into the White House, Chip said with a smile, "The hall is bigger than our mobile home."

The young Carters soon found that their new quarters came with history built in. The personal furnishings for their apartments were to be selected from the government warehouse in Alexandria, Virginia. Chip and Caron found a chest of drawers used by President Truman, and Jeff and Annette chose Abraham Lincoln's chair and Thomas Jefferson's inkstand.

Back in Plains during preelection days Chip had told reporters that he didn't ever want to live in the White House should his father win the presidency. Now he says that "the thing that changed our minds was living in Plains and the thousands of tourists. They're looking for Carters. Unrealistically, we dreamed we could go back to Plains [after the campaign] and have the same life we had before. One morning it took me an hour and a half to get there [to the Carter family peanut warehouse where he worked] because of tourists. So we decided to leave."

Of White House living, he commented, "When we go to the South Lawn, people aren't standing there bothering us. In Plains we had forty to fifty people a day knocking at the front door. Here, that doesn't happen."

*　　*　　*

During their first days as White House residents, Caron, in spite of her advanced pregnancy, substituted for mother-in-law Rosalynn twice. The first time was to welcome a delegation of Georgia librarians, the second to attend a luncheon the Wolftrap Associates, a group that provides financial support for the Wolftrap Center for the Performing Arts in Virginia. Caron said that, after her child was born, she would "really like to get involved in some of the projects Rosalynn will be working on."

All Rosalynn's daughters-in-law are on excellent terms with her. They echo her keen interest in the aged, mental health, and women's rights. In Caron's case, this remained true even after the White House announced, on November 13, 1978, that Chip and Caron Carter were separating. The announcement ended months of rumors. It was particularly sad for Rosalynn and Jimmy, who have always stressed the old fashioned virtues of marriage and family life. Rosalynn was often seen with Chip and Caron's baby son, James Earl Carter IV, playing around the White House grounds.

In making the announcement of the breakup, Rosalynn's press secretary, Mary Hoyt, said that Chip and Caron "know that their friends respect their decision to make no further public comment." "We are all going to miss that baby so much," Mrs. Hoyt added. The Carter's eleven-month-old grandson returned to live with his mother in her native Hawkinsville, Ga.

*   *   *

After the move to Washington, Jeff became the first family's official photographer. His work drew immediate praise. His family groups, such as Amy sitting on her father's knee just before bedtime, displayed a great sense of intimacy and charm. His big moment was the wedding of Uncle Billy's second daughter Jalna to Johnny Theus of Ellaville, Georgia, May 13, 1978. The event took place at the Billy Carter home just outside Plains. Jeff made a record of the event for some of the biggest magazines and newspapers in the country. The wedding had all the flamboyance that has brought brother Billy so much attention in the press, and nephew Jeff captured it all on film, even the styrofoam swans that glided under a fairytale bridal bridge that spanned Uncle Billy and Aunt Sybil's swimming pool. Jeff even caught the surprise in his parents and Miss Lillian's eyes as they watched the nuptial swans glide by.

The pet parakeet that Jeff and Annette brought with them when they moved to the White House attracted a great deal of attention in the press. Although birds have long been traditional pets in high places, Jeff and Annette's parakeet is probably the most famous bird to live in the White House since Dolly Madison's macaw.

*   *   *

Rosalynn and Miss Lillian are very much persons in their own right. Long before Rosalynn ever dreamed of becoming First Lady, Miss Lillian was out doing what no other wealthy white Plains lady would do: nursing the poor, black and white. She then became a Peace Corps worker when other women her age would be several years retired.

Since Jimmy became President, in spite of advancing years (she is past 80), Miss Lillian has a splendid record of services rendered as a delegate from the United States at such functions as the funeral of the late Pope Paul. She is devoted to all her family and they to her. She has been quoted many times as saying what splendid daughters-in-law she has (Rosalynn and Sybil).

If anything, her record of public service has always been an inspiration to our now First Lady. During the Presidential campaign certain journalists were eager to make up some kind of family feud between Miss Lillian and Rosalynn. To this false accusation, Miss Lillian had the perfect grandmotherly reply:

"Would she have left Amy with me for two years of campaigning if she didn't like me?"

Following Billy Carter's much-publicized anti-Semitic remarks said to have been made at the time that a delegation of Libyans were visiting him, Rosalynn Carter became the first of the family to disagree with him publicly.

Said the First Lady in no uncertain terms: "I disagree with some of the things he [Billy] says and so does Jimmy."

At the same time she made mention of the then-current investigation of the Carter peanut warehouse. Rosalynn said that she did not believe a grand jury investigating these records and the warehouse loans from the National Bank of Georgia would find any wrongdoing.

Rosalynn kept the books at the warehouse until she turned them over to Sybil Carter, Billy's wife, in 1970. "I left them in very good hands," Rosalynn was quick to say, adding: "Our income tax has been checked every year since Jimmy came home from the Navy."

Rosalynn has always maintained a pleasant, friendly relationship with brother Billy, meeting for family events such as the annual Christmas morning breakfast at Miss Lillian's, but otherwise they live in different worlds. Rosalynn is quiet, meticulous about everything, and deeply religious, while Billy is fun-loving, outgoing, and criticized by the church folk in Plains for his beer and bourbon drinking.

*　　*　　*

At her first State Dinner, which was for President José López Portillo of Mexico, Amy sat between her parents quietly reading a mystery story. At her second, for Canadian Prime Minister Pierre Trudeau, she was seated next to Senator Edmund Muskie of Maine, who encouraged her with "eat your spinach." This time Amy was reading *The Story of the Gettysburg Address*. She was allowed to bring books to read at the State Dinners in case she got restless.

It became increasingly evident that there was only a minimum degree of the usual pomp and ceremony in the new Carter White House. On certain points Rosalynn had disagreed with Jimmy. "I don't think 'Ruffles and Flourishes' and 'Hail to the Chief' ought to be played here in the White House," he argued. "I'm a civilian president of a democratic country. I think the only time they should be played is when I'm on a military base and acting as Commander-in-Chief. But Rosalynn disagrees. She maintains that "people expect a show of respect for the office itself. Now, that's an honest difference of opinion, and so far we haven't resolved it."

The Mexican President and his wife, a close friend of Rosalynn's, were served shrimp gumbo. It was prepared by White House chef Henry Haller, who has cooked for State Dinners and the First Family of each succeeding administration since he was engaged by Lady Bird Johnson. Lyndon had been complaining of Jackie Kennedy's French chef, whose cooking did not suit his rugged Texan stomach.

Rosalynn and the White House social secretary, Gretchen Poston, also selected the menu for the Canadian visitors, this time Alaskan crab. Although she had been to the United States before, this was Margaret Trudeau's first State Visit; and since she separated from her husband shortly afterwards, it was probably her last.

*   *   *

For the State Dinner for British Prime Minister and Mrs. James Callaghan, John Ficklin, the maitre d', who first began working at the White House under President Harry Truman, set out the Morgantown crystal, the King Charles silver, and the Truman administration china. Each guest's name was inscribed by the calligraphers on seating cards, an old White House tradition.

The Callaghans were served roast beef and Yorkshire pudding. Rosalynn made up the guest list herself as usual. Some of the guests were pleasantly surprised to receive invitations, for, as Rosalynn said, "We just try to think of people we know in the country. At the last dinner we had a couple from North Carolina who run a little store."

Rosalynn particularly enjoyed the British Prime Minister and his wife. A delightful touch at that dinner were the violet nosegays Rosalynn had thought up for the ladies. "It made me feel I was really welcome," said one of the guests.

The reception following the State Dinner for the Callaghans, who, like the Carters, are Baptists, was especially notable. Rosalynn borrowed a 125-year-old square grand piano from the Smithsonian for the young singers, Jan De Gaetani, a mezzo-soprano, and Robert White, a tenor. White's rendering in Welsh of "All Through the Night" almost brought the house down.

*　　*　　*

Rusty (Elmer) Young is the chief floral designer at the Executive Mansion, where he has worked since 1953. He says that former First Lady Jacqueline Kennedy Onassis trained him in the art of flower arranging. With his small staff, he is busiest when there is an official function like a State Dinner.

Dedicated Garden Club volunteers are a frequent source of flowers for White House functions, and sometimes the flowers come from old discarded gardens that the owners allow Young to search. When flowers are donated to the White House from citizens' own gardens, Rosalynn always writes them a thank you note. On other occasions, in keeping with Rosalynn's desire for thrift, Young visits local flower markets for bargains. Although all the state rooms need constant flowers for the benefit of the tourists who visit them, Rosalynn cut down on the flowers for the family quarters. She likes flowers in Amy's bedroom and the one she shares with Jimmy, in the Center Hall, and as their dining table centerpiece.

Each First Lady seems to have preferred a different fashion for White House floral arrangements. Mamie Eisenhower preferred only her favorite gladioli, and Jackie Kennedy brought in the informal nosegay arrangement made up of many varieties. For the visit of Queen Elizabeth II and Prince Philip, Betty Ford chose carloads of wild flowers. The Queen Anne's lace gave an almost ghostly, ethereal effect to the moonlit Rose Garden where the royal party was held. Rosalynn Carter's most memorable excursion into floral decoration may have come on the occasion of her entertaining the wives of all the Latin American dignitaries who were in Washington for the signing of the Panama Canal treaty. The ladies were all treated to a floating luncheon aboard a 103-foot-long Wilson Line boat that took them up the Potomac to Mount Vernon. That day Rusty Young and his helpers garlanded the boat with laurel, carnations, and hanging baskets of red geraniums, a monumental task.

*   *   *

When their family food bill for ten days during their first two weeks in the White House came to $600, Rosalynn was horrified. "When they came in," said chef Haller, who came to the White House from New York's Ambassador

Hotel," I didn't know they wanted to eat leftovers, so I served maybe roast beef twice a week and tenderloin of beef. Then I was told to cut that down . . . We don't want to spend this kind of money."

"They want to use up everything possible," he added. When Rosalynn found a left-over sweet-and-sour cabbage dish in the refrigerator she told him to serve it for lunch.

Haller says that nowadays there is a definite southern touch to the First Family meals. He cooks their sea trout breaded and fried crisp just as they like it; then he serves it with spoon bread or hush puppies. Grits, collard greens, and cornbread patties are regulars on the menu. "They only eat dessert on Sundays," says Haller. The Carters pay for their own food.

Each Monday Haller sends Rosalynn family menus for a week, and he says that she "is easy to please." He also notes that "the Carters are very punctual about meals, which for a chef is very important."

For official functions chef Haller uses his large, gleaming, stainless steel kitchen. He prepares the First Family meals in their modern kitchen complete with a four-burner, two-oven gas stove and a dishwasher, refrigerator, and freezer. Supper, the main meal of the day (Rosalynn refuses to call it "dinner"), was often attended by the two younger Carter sons and their wives, who lived in small apartments on the third floor.

_16_

FOR Allie Smith, who became an instant celebrity when her daughter became First Lady, the election brought changes. No longer can she leave her front door unlocked, and for the first time in her life she has found the need for an unlisted telephone number. Tourist buses stop and point out her neat beige clapboard house with the gray porch and the rocking chair where Miss Allie used to like to sit. She has lived in the house for nearly fifty years.

Miss Allie was also one of the first parking ticket casualties in Plains. It was Christmas Eve, 1976, her seventy-first birthday, and she was out doing some last minute holiday shopping. Rosalynn, Jimmy and all the family were coming for dinner the next day. She finally found an empty space for her car, and upon her return from the stores, discovered that she had been given a ticket for parking next to a fire hydrant. Miss Allie took it philosophically:

"I can't complain. My son warned me to be more careful with all this extra traffic. I shouldn't have parked there. I've always believed we have to pay for our mistakes."

*   *   *

At her son-in-law's Inauguration, she was given the Lincoln Bedroom to sleep in. Years before at Harry Truman's it had been offered to his mother, sprightly Martha Young Truman, another Southerner. Mrs. Truman declined with the words, "No, thank you. I would rather be dead."

Rosalynn told her mother to be sure and look out for the ghost that went with the room. Miss Allie promised that she would. "The next morning mother said she had slept like a top, even though the experience of being in that historic room was unbelievably exciting," Rosalynn recalls. Miss Lillian spent the same night in the Queen's Bedroom at the White House. "Where I belong," said she.

When Miss Allie returned to Plains from Washington, she felt somewhat sad, for the thought came over her that she would not be able to slip over to Rosalynn's house and visit. She was also concerned about her daughter's personal safety now that she was First Lady. And she worried about Amy. "I'm afraid she'll never know what it's like to be an ordinary little girl again."

When her son Murray, 42, a lay preacher at Plains Methodist Church, was divorced from his wife, Frances, he went home to live with his mother. Miss Allie enjoyed cooking and washing for him all over again. She still remained on good terms with her former daughter-in-law, Frances, who calls her "the best of mother-in-laws." "She still invites me to eat with her when she cooks rutabagas for supper," says Frances appreciatively.

Murray, who was only eight years old when his father died, credits his mother for his good Christian upbringing and for instilling in him his love for religion and churchwork. He recalls with a broad smile all the spankings Miss Allie gave him "for my own good." "Mother really disciplined us. She spanked us all with a peach switch. It did hurt, but I was bad and those spankings taught me the difference between right and wrong."

When, in August 1977, Murray remarried in the same church where his famous sister had herself been a bride, she returned with her husband, the President of the United States, for the ceremony.

*   *   *

Miss Lillian's home in town and her beloved Pond House out in the country are both inevitable stops for all the tour buses. The former has signs on the front lawn . . .

NO ADMITTANCE

but there is still no fence. In contrast, a high mesh one guards the entrance to the Pond House with signs that read:

NO PARKING . . . MOVE ON

By contrast, Martha Truman and her devoted daughter and life-long companion, Mary Jane Truman, refused to allow the Secret Service to build a high fence around their family home in Independence, Missouri. "It isn't neighborly," they said.

*   *   *

Miss Lillian has fulfilled a number of important engagements "for Jimmy's sake" since he became President. She has proved a splendid goodwill ambassador in the way that Princess Margaret was in her youth for her sister, Queen Elizabeth. Like Princess Margaret in those carefree years, Miss Lillian has "the common touch."

With her grandson Chip, Miss Lillian led the United States delegation at the funeral of India's President Fak-

135

huddin Ali Ahmed. It was an inspired choice to send her to the land where she had labored with the Peace Corps a decade before. In her black dress, Miss Lillian listened to the simple prayer offered for the deceased: "From God we came and unto God we return."

In Ireland as part of her son's family-to-family Friendship Exchange, Miss Lillian was in good mettle. She told Irish reporters that Jimmy's energy program woes had him at rather a low point. She then added emphatically, "He'll overcome it. Jimmy's always right. He has aged a bit, but I don't worry. Neither does he. He once told me, 'I asked for it, and now I have got it, and I can handle it.' "

The President's mother was treated right royally in the Land of the Green. She even got to sit in the enormous royal chair in Dublin Castle's State Apartment. Her legs were too short to reach the floor, and she was given a velvet topped footstool on which to rest them.

Miss Lillian never was a woman to mince words. In September 1978, she told an audience at Emporia State University in Kansas that her Jimmy was "the greatest man on earth."

*   *   *

Rosalynn was especially happy when her son Chip accompanied a congressional delegation on a good will mission to China, arriving in Peking on April 9, 1977. He was not the first American President's offspring to be a guest of the Chinese government. Julie and David Eisenhower were special visitors after President Nixon had opened diplomatic relations with Peking in 1972.

*   *   *

At home in the White House, First Child Amy Carter continued to do well in school, quite oblivious to the Secret

Service men who were sent to guard her. Rosalynn and Jimmy were fully aware of the dangers that could beset their beloved daughter. Susan Ford, only daughter of former President Ford, had hated the constant presence of her bodyguards, but then she was a teenager.

Because of poor vision, Amy at first wore large-rimmed, thick eyeglasses. Later, like her mother, she began experimenting with contact lenses. Rosalynn does not like wearing regular glasses in public, although she does wear them in the privacy of her office. She says that contact lenses "are great for speeches."

*   *   *

To other children who write her, Amy sends a postcard bearing her picture on one side. Her reply usually reads:

Thank you for writing to me. It's fun living in the White House and I am glad you are my friend.

Amy Carter.

Or
Thank you for your letter. Washington is fun. I play with my dog, Grits, and my cat, Misty, and I've made lots of new friends.

Love,
Amy Carter

Each facsimile letter includes Amy's exclusive portrait of Misty.

*   *   *

During the summer vacation of 1977, Amy took part in a special four-day-a-week "enrichment program" at George Washington University's reading center. The children's job was to read and compile handbooks on transportation. They took special field trips, including a float down the Chesapeake and Ohio Canal on a mule-drawn barge and visits to Washington's Air and Space Museum.

When asked what were Amy's special qualifications to be included in the highly selective group, the program's directors said that they felt she showed a "strong potential for leadership."

*   *   *

From December 7 until the holidays, the Carters received an average of five hundred Christmas cards a day from their fellow Americans. Among the unusual gifts that were delivered was a chain saw and the offer of two others for Amy. The chain saw was returned.

A news report had appeared saying that Amy had told a friend that a chain saw was what she wanted for Christmas. Explained Mary Finch Hoyt, Rosalynn's press secretary, "I think Amy might have said *train set*, not *chain saw*."

Rosalynn had so many requests for the recipe of Jimmy's favorite cheese ring that she finally released it beautifully scripted on a card bearing a drawing of the White House.

Jimmy lit the nation's permanent Christmas tree on the Ellipse just south of the White House. A thirty-two-foot spruce, it replaced the previous year's "permanent" tree, which was rotting and was later used as a yule log. The new tree was given by a husband and wife from a suburb of Potomac, Maryland, who had had it growing on their lawn for twenty-five years.

"Plains Special" Cheese Ring

1 pound grated sharp cheese	Black pepper
1 cup finely chopped nuts	Dash cayenne
1 cup mayonnaise	Strawberry preserves, optional
1 small onion, finely grated	

Combine all ingredients except preserves, season to taste with pepper. Mix well and place in a 5 or 6 cup lightly greased ring mold. Refrigerate until firm for several hours or overnight.

To serve, unmold, and if desired, fill center with strawberry preserves, or serve plain with crackers.

With best wishes, Rosalynn Carter

Rosalynn's "very, very special" Christmas tree stood twenty feet tall in the Blue Room of the White House. It came from the State of Washington's forest at Spirit Lake. Saying that "commercialism has tainted the nation's Christmas spirit," the First Lady proudly showed off her tree hung with fifteen hundred decorations made by retarded citizens. The theme, at Rosalynn and Jimmy's request, was "American Classic." At the First Lady's invitation, Mark Hampton, the prestigious New York decorator, coordinated the White House Christmas decorations.

As usual, the family spent Christmas at home in Plains, where, on December 7, a very windy day, Rosalynn had dedicated a much needed state tourist information center. Jimmy told reporters, "See you after Christmas," as he disappeared into the family home.

From Rosalynn, Jimmy received a woolen jacket which she had had his mother buy on her Irish trip. "Jimmy said he wanted one for his fireside television chats," Rosalynn explained.

Miss Lillian gave Rosalynn a beige slip with matching accessories and Amy a special ski cap and scarf. Billy Carter received the most unusual gift, a pinball machine from his wife.

Scrambled eggs, grits and sausage—the Carter clan's traditional Christmas morning breakfast—was again held at Miss Lillian's. Dinner was at Miss Allie's.

*   *   *

Jimmy and Rosalynn were soon back in Plains for another family occasion. Alton Carter, the head of the family, died in the Americus and Sumter County Hospital on January 18, 1978, aged 89 years. He had been in business in Plains for seventy-four of these.

Jimmy and Rosalynn accompanied Miss Lillian to the funeral service in the Maranatha Baptist Church. Said Don Carter, Vice-President of the Knight-Ridder Newspapers, Miami, Florida, of his father: "He was a man of great strength and character, and I loved him."

Uncle Buddy was just about the most respected man in Plains.

Rosalynn and Jimmy Carter assist his mother, Miss Lillian, as they arrive for the funeral of Alton Carter. *Wide World Photos*

_17_

R OBERT Redford is Rosalynn's favorite movie star, while her ever young mother-in-law, Miss Lillian, prefers Paul Newman. Jimmy's favorites are veteran actors Henry Fonda and Gregory Peck.

The President and First Lady were only casual moviegoers before living in the White House. Now with their own projection room they enjoy the latest motion picture offerings. The projectionist for the movie room in the East Wing typically gets the films the Carters select on twenty-four-hour notice. Their first choices were *The Godfather*, *Rocky*, *All the President's Men*, which was about the Watergate scandal that ended the Nixon administration, and *Network*.

Both Rosalynn and Jimmy enjoy the theater, and during his first four months in office, they visited the John F. Kennedy Center for Performing Arts no less than seven times. Each evening patrons in all three of the center's theaters looked eagerly to see if the Presidential Seal was hung on the Presidential Box to announce the First Family's imminent arrival. Although Jimmy's two immediate predecessors, Richard Nixon and Gerald Ford, each attended performances in the center only twice during their entire terms of office, the Carters more than made up for them.

Twice in those early months of Jimmy's administration Rosalynn went on her own, once to see the musical *Annie* and then again to catch Shirley MacLaine's revue. One Sunday afternoon in February 1977, Rosalynn and Jimmy slipped quietly off to see an excellent performance of *Madama Butterfly* given by the Opera Society of Washington. They did not tell the press, and there were some ruffled feelings next day. They were trying to show that when they needed a little cultural relaxation, it was not a media event.

The Carters also visited the Kennedy Center for the New York City Ballet's production of "A Midsummer Night's Dream," Hal Holbrook's enchanting "Mark Twain Tonight," and for the cello recital by Matislav Rostropovich, remaining for two encores. Jimmy and Rosalynn both love classical music so much that Jimmy has it taped into the Oval Office.

Of course, Roger Stevens, the hard working director of the Kennedy Center for the Performing Arts, was delighted by their so-frequent presence. "They come so often, and sometimes with so little advance notice," he said, "it's no longer necessary to go out and meet them at the door. It adds a great deal of interest and zest to see the President and First Lady in their box. It adds glamor to the performance, and the performers appreciate it when they come backstage. We appreciate it very much that he has said several times he enjoys coming here and expects to continue."

*   *   *

Rosalynn is no novice when it comes to the stage. Novelist Norman Mailer is on record as saying that she could have been "a movie star of a waitress in a good 1930s film—the sort who gives you cheer about the future of the human

144

condition." She proved herself by an impressive narration of Aaron Copland's "A Lincoln Portrait" before an audience of two thousand in Washington's Constitution Hall. Leonard Bernstein conducted a full symphony orchestra, and, although Rosalynn had neither read the text nor the score until the dress rehearsal, she acquitted herself like a seasoned trouper. Afterwards, to resounding applause, she whispered, "Can you believe I did that?"

*   *   *

It was only fitting that, early in 1977, America's new First Lady should make her first official visit to New York to meet the First Lady of American music—the great Marian Anderson. The occasion was a seventy-fifth birthday concert in honor of the contralto who some twenty years before became the first black soloist at the Metropolitan Opera House.

Rosalynn and Miss Anderson sat together in a first-tier box at Carnegie Hall during the performance. Many recalled that it was another First Lady, Eleanor Roosevelt, whom Rosalynn greatly admires, who supported the renowned singer when the Daughters of the American Revolution banned her from singing in Washington's Constitution Hall. Mrs. Roosevelt immediately resigned her membership in the organization. On the morning of Jimmy's Inauguration, Miss Anderson sang before 75,000 people in front of the Lincoln Memorial in Washington.

The Carnegie Hall tribute included songs that had highlighted the Anderson career for more than half a century. Rosalynn gave the First Lady of American Music the President's personal birthday wishes together with news of a Congressional Resolution authorizing the United States Treasury to strike a gold medal in her honor.

Miss Anderson, with her devoted husband, Orpheus Fisher, lives quietly in Danbury, Connecticut. Frail and in poor health, she was visibly touched by the evening's events, especially when Mayor Abe Beame presented her with the Handel Medallion for cultural contributions to "the city, the country, and the world."

In October 1978, President Carter presented the Congressional gold medal to Miss Anderson. The medal had been authorized by Congress nearly two years before, and when Jimmy accidentally dropped it as he was in the process of handing it to Miss Anderson, she said with a laugh, "I have waited so long I thought it might have to be presented posthumously."

*   *   *

On August 8, 1978, Jimmy and Rosalynn were back in New York City for a special ceremony. The 389th Army Band played "Happy Days Are Here Again" as the President signed the bill authorizing the $1.65 billion Federal loan guarantee that would help New York City cope with its fiscal problems.

"I am proud of this greatest of cities," declared Jimmy as he sat down at an antique mahogany desk used by George Washington. After he had signed the bill before an estimated crowd of four thousand and some two thousand invited guests, the band struck up "Give My Regards to Broadway."

That evening Jimmy and Rosalynn were joined by Mayor Edward I. Koch, Bess Myerson, Governor Hugh L. Carey, and the latter's friend, Ann Ford Uzielli, for a visit to the Longacre Theater. There they enjoyed the hit show, *Ain't Misbehavin'*—an all black revue featuring the jazz tunes of the legendary Fats Waller. Afterwards the Presidential party enjoyed a dinner party at the United States Steak House in the Time-Life Building which lasted two hours.

Jimmy and Rosalynn both said they wanted to eat dinner "in a real restaurant with real people" and not in a separate party room. They sat at a large round table in the center of the room. Rosalynn, wearing an elegant V-necked black gown, was radiant that evening. Both she and the President ate Chateaubriand steak served with mixed green salad and Roquefort dressing. Neither wanted the cream of peanut soup.

Hot fudge sundae was the dessert, a perfect choice for Jimmy's well known sweet tooth. Mayor Koch paid the check.

*   *   *

Another favorite of the Carters is singer Willie Nelson. When they heard he was performing with Emmylou Harris at the Merriweather Post Pavilion in Columbia, Maryland, they helicoptered down from Camp David to enjoy the show. Jimmy was in shirtsleeves; Rosalynn in a white pants suit. It was an informal, happy occasion with Willie giving all he had to his own interpretation of "Georgia on My Mind."

Rosalynn had to stand in for Jimmy when Nelson came to play on the White House lawn in September 1978. Jimmy calls himself Willie's 'Number One Fan,' who had personally invited Nelson to the party he had arranged for members of the National Association for Stock Car Auto Racing, but was otherwise engaged with President Sadat of Egypt and Prime Minister Begin of Israel at Camp David. Jimmy is also a stock racing car buff from way back.

"Up Against the Wall, Redneck Mother" nearly brought down the Executive Mansion. However, the hit of the day was a duet sung by Willie Nelson, baritone, and Rosalynn Carter, soprano.

*   *   *

Among the many show business people invited to the White House by the First Family were Archie and Edith Bunker, in real life, Carroll O'Connor and Jean Stapleton, who had just received Emmy Awards for their performances in the long-running *All in the Family* television show. Archie was unable to attend the White House party given in the show's honor because he was receiving treatment for high blood pressure, but he managed to participate in the festivities by means of a telephone hookup.

Archie and Edith's favorite chairs were presented to the Smithsonian for posterity. "It's better than being cast in wax," said Edith. In all her wildest domestic dreams, Edith Bunker, the loyal, long-suffering housewife never thought she would one day be hugged by the President of the United States—and his First Lady was delighted.

*   *   *

With Second Lady, Joan Mondale, a talented potter, to help her, Rosalynn selected the finest American hand-crafted pottery and glassware for the traditional Senate wives' luncheon. Included was the work of Lewis and Risa Dimm, craftsmen at Livingston Pottery in New York State. The young potters were honored that it was their work Mrs. Carter chose for her own table.

For five years the Dimms have worked in an insulated and sheet-rocked barn behind their circa 1790 house. Says Lewis of their rural location, "This is not an especially good place for a potter to work. We'd like to have more of a retail business here, but there isn't the traffic, so we sell mainly wholesale."

Wholesale or not, Rosalynn Carter's recognition of their work will always be the highlight of their joint careers.

Rosalynn addressing the 18th annual United Press International Editors Conference in Puerto Rico. *Wide World Photos*

_18_

"I think I am the person closest to the President of the United States, and if I can help him understand the countries of the world, then that's what I intend to do."

This, her eyes flashing angrily, was Rosalynn Carter's reply to an American television reporter who had dared to ask just what made her believe she was fit to discuss serious matters with heads of state. The First Lady had undergone twenty-six hours of special briefings on Latin America and the Caribbean to prepare her for the 13-day visit to Jamaica, Costa Rica, Ecuador, Peru, Brazil, Colombia, and Venezuela. Zbigniew Brzezinski, the President's National Security Adviser, was among the forty experts who instructed her.

Latin American diplomats were somewhat skeptical of her mission. In their countries a woman's place is still considered to be in the home. But President Carter described his wife as a "political partner of mine," one who would "conduct substantive talks with the leaders of those countries and bring back a report on how we might strengthen our ties."

A White House aide explained it this way: "Jimmy wants to show these countries that he cares about them and is interested in their problems. In his mind, the best way he could do that—short of making the trip himself—was to send Rosalynn."

*   *   *

After spending the Memorial Day weekend together on St. Simon's Island, Jimmy and Amy bid Rosalynn bon voyage at Brunswick Airport as she left for Jamaica on an Air Force Boeing 707 called "Executive First Family." She was accompanied by a party of nineteen, excluding nine Secret Service agents and representatives of the press. Terence A. Todman, Assistant Secretary of State for Inter-American Affairs, was on hand to assist her. There were also her personal hairdresser and a White House nurse. Rosalynn's new monogram was on all the baggage and press kits.

Rosalynn affectionately stroked Amy's long blonde hair before boarding the plane. The little girl looked sad standing barefoot in shorts and a sleeveless blouse. As her mother's plane took off, Jimmy lifted Amy into his arms and carried her like a baby. Then, en route back to Washington with Amy's nurse, Mary Fitzpatrick, carrying a large shoulder bag, the President and Amy stopped off in Plains for a brief visit. On hand to meet them was Miss Lillian in bell-bottomed slacks and Scott Roberson, 9, who presented Amy with a foot-high stack of comic books.

Amy seemed very pleased to see Scott, greeting him even before she did her grandmother, who said with a smile: "That's her boyfriend. They have just always been sweethearts."

The President strolled down the main street of Plains greeting old neighbors, tourists, and his boyhood nurse,

Rachael Clark, to whom he gave a big hug. Later he went with brother Billy to pick wild plums on one of the family farms.

*   *   *

Arriving in Jamaica, the First Lady was met by the Prime Minister, Michael Manley. The skies were overcast, but this did not dim the sincerity of her official welcome. The Prime Minister said that he hoped his country would "gain in understanding of the new directions of United States policy" during her twenty-four-hour visit.

Replying to his greeting, Rosalynn, speaking in a firm clear voice said: "Our countries have a long tradition of warm friendship, and you have roused the admiration of our country by your democratic achievements. We want to consult closely with you and strengthen our ties of friendship as you strive for more social and economic justice. I know that you are aware that what you are doing here in Jamaica has great significance not only for Jamaica, but for the developing world."

The twenty-minute ride from the airport to Prime Minister Hanley's official residence was typically West Indian and spontaneously joyful. On the way the motorcade halted long enough for Rosalynn and the Prime Minister to greet hundreds of cheering, flag-waving school children, while a loudspeaker blared, "Welcome to Jamaica." So dense was the throng that Secret Service agents had to help Mrs. Carter back into her car.

She visited two social service centers in a poor section of Kingston and delighted everybody with the very special way she has with children. Eleven-year-old Paulette Aron, with a large pink bow in her hair, ran towards Rosalynn, hugged her tightly, and then walked proudly beside her. She also met with Peace Corps volunteers, visited a sugar co-operative, and attended a dinner given in her honor by the Prime Minister.

She talked with the Prime Minister for several hours, insisting that America's policy towards Cuba was changing at last. Manley is a long-time admirer of that country. Four days later, the White House announced its plans for a limited exchange of diplomats with Cuba.

Before leaving for Costa Rica, the second stop of her seven-nation tour, Rosalynn told reporters that she was "very much impressed" by the Jamaican Prime Minister. "He really hurts for people who lack food and clothing and housing," she said.

Asked how he personally rated the wife of the American President as a diplomat, Manley replied: "First class. I can't put it higher than that. She was very knowledgeable, very charming, and very direct."

*　　*　　*

While Rosalynn was on tour, second son Chip and his wife Caron were in London for the Silver Jubilee celebrations of Queen Elizabeth II. They dined with the Queen and Prince Philip at the Guild Hall, lunched with Prince Charles at Buckingham Palace, and dined with Princess Anne and her husband, Captain Mark Phillips. At the same time, Rosalynn's youngest son, Jeff, was in Yucatan looking at archaeological ruins with friends for what was officially called a five-day private visit.

*　　*　　*

In Costa Rica, Rosalynn listened to President Daniel Oduber Quiros sympathetically when he asked that the United States raise its beef imports quota. "I could not promise anything that we could not deliver," Rosalynn re-

154

plied. Marjorie Oduber, Costa Rica's First Lady, knew of Rosalynn's long-time interest in folk dancing and took her to watch a colorful exhibition of Ecuadorian dancing.

Mrs. Carter encountered some heckling in Quito, Ecuador, when students shouted, "Rosalynn Carter, go home" and "Bloody Rosalynn." The 9,350-foot-high altitude proved taxing to the First Lady, who seemed tired. She was given two doses of oxygen. Recovered, she announced to the ruling military triumvirate that her country did not expect to lift the trade restrictions it had imposed when Ecuador, with other OPEC members, had raised its oil prices.

The Ecuadorians then told her that they thought the U.S.A. should lift the ban that prevented them from buying Israeli-made Kfir jet planes, which are equipped with engines manufactured by General Electric.

Rosalynn told them that the sale had been stopped because her husband's administration did not want the responsibility of introducing sophisticated weapons into Latin America. The Ecuadorian leaders insisted that they needed the jets because their neighbor and old enemy, Peru, already possessed the latest in fighting equipment.

As they continued their talks in the Legislative Palace, Rosalynn could not fail to hear more student yelling, "Imperialist Rosalynn Carter" and the now too familiar slogan "Yankee Imperialism." On her departure, the demonstrators could get no nearer than one hundred yards to her motorcade. Two Molotov cocktails were thrown, and the police retaliated with tear gas.

*　　*　　*

Arriving in fabled Peru, land of the Incas, Rosalynn met for nearly three hours of private talks with President Francisco Morales Bermúdez. In her quiet, Southern manner, she said that she wished her hosts could slow the pace of their military buildup, which was upsetting the Ecuadorians.

She was taken to visit an irrigation project and a potato center, and, as a farmer's wife, she could talk from experience on both subjects. She then spent a weekend resting at Granja Azul.

Half way through her goodwill tour Rosalynn said that she did not think that the male leaders of Latin America had treated her any differently or held anything back in their discussions because she was a woman. "Almost in every case," said Rosalynn, "when we start talking with these people and they will say, 'I don't know exactly how to say it,' I'll say, 'Listen, you can be blunt—just be blunt.' And after that, they're blunt."

"I really believe that my trip has been valuable to these leaders, too, because they don't know Jimmy. Just the fact that he cares enough about Latin America to send me to talk with them, I think means a lot to them."

Every day Rosalynn reported details of her trip to Jimmy by telephone. She relayed the several invitations she had received from Latin-American leaders for him to visit their countries.

* * *

What was termed the First Lady's toughest challenge and sternest test as a visiting dignitary came next. Brazil was far from pleased with the American President's attempting to stop West Germany from supplying Brazil with the technology to set up nuclear power stations. They were equally unhappy with his criticism of what he considered to be their human rights violations.

Brazilian President Ernesto Geisel received Rosalynn politely. He was impressed with the forthright manner in which she answered his sometimes pointed questions.

In Colombia, she discussed ways of stopping the smuggling of $500 million worth of drugs into the United States each year, and President Alfonso López Michelsen promised to do what he could.

In Caracas, Venezuela, Rosalynn was in the Presidential Palace attending a meeting with Mrs. Bianquita Rodriguez de Perez, the wife of President Carlos Andres Perez, when she suffered a sudden attack of nausea. She had to lie down for nearly an hour and was then forced to cancel a scheduled meeting with the country's labor leaders. The previous day she had been involved in discussions with Venezuela's President to examine the gap between industrialized and nonindustrialized nations.

*   *   *

Landing at Andrew Air Force Base upon her return home, Rosalynn was met by the President, Vice-President Mondale, her daughter Amy, Secretary of State Cyrus Vance, and several Latin American Ambassadors.

Although she looked pale and tired, the First Lady made a little speech in which she said that the President of Venezuela had told her that her visit had done much to improve relations between their two countries. She continued to say that the old attitude of paternalism had been broken down by the new administration's policy of personal visits. She had begun her address with the delightful . . . "Mr. President . . . Jimmy."

The President drew laughter, especially from the Vice-President, when he said that it had been more of a sacrifice to send his wife to Latin America "than it would have been to send anyone else including the Vice-President."

Looking back on her foreign travels Rosalynn recently said, "I've learned that people are people. They're the

157

same everywhere. If you're friendly and interested, that's enough."

*   *   *

In January of 1978, on a raw, cold morning following a night of storms, Rosalynn stood beside Jimmy at Poland's Tomb of the Unknown Warrior. With her head swatched in a scarf, she gazed at the brilliant reds and whites of the Presidential wreath. Then she was off alone for a walk through Warsaw's Old City. Her visit delighted the hundreds of Poles she met along the way and who cheered and clapped their hands.

With Polish-born Zbigniew Brzezinski, the United States National Security Adviser, as translator, she visited for ninety minutes with Catholic prelate Stefan Cardinal Wyszynski. Dressed all in blue, Rosalynn struck a responsive chord in the seventy-six-year-old patriot, who presented her with two rosaries, one for herself and the other to give to Brzezinski's mother, then living in Canada and in her eighties.

It was the first major foreign tour for the Carters, and Poland was just the beginning. At Rosalynn's special request, with all the glitter of the *Arabian Nights*, Jimmy and Rosalynn spent New Year's Eve at a State dinner given by the Shah of Iran and his Empress in Tehran. In India, they felt a special bond because of Miss Lillian's service with the Peace Corps. About fifteen miles from New Delhi, they visited the village of Daulatpur, renamed for the occasion "Carter-Poori" (Carter's Place). There they received the red, Hindu *tilak* mark on their foreheads. Rosalynn had to bend low to allow a child clad in a crimson sari to etch out the symbol with her finger.

In Saudi Arabia, Rosalynn, well known for her stand on Women's Rights, found herself in a country where, until that time, King Khalid's Queen had never appeared in public during her husband's reign. However, although Rosalynn was excluded along with the other women from attending the State Dinner given by the King, Queen Sitta gave a dinner in Rosalynn's honor in another room. It would be interesting to know what the two women talked about.

The Carters landed in Aswan, Egypt for a visit that lasted only fifty-nine minutes and that became famous as "The Pocket Summit." A chill wind was blowing over the desert as military band played The Anniversary Waltz. Presidents Sadat and Carter talked together in the Aswan Airport Terminal lounge while the two First Ladies visited together.

Flying on to France, Jimmy and Rosalynn were given a rousing welcome by French citizens and President Valéry Giscard d'Estaing. It was reminiscent of the welcome once given to President Kennedy. The Carters were intrigued with the fabled Palace of Versailles, especially the ill-fated Marie Antoinette's bedroom. They were late for the reception in their honor, which in itself was most unusual for the ever punctual President. The Paris newspaper *Le Monde* commented with tongue in cheek, "The Hall of Mirrors has not known such a brawl since revolutionary days."

During a brief seven-hour visit with Belgum's King Baudouin and Queen Fabiola, Jimmy became the first American President ever to visit the European Commission in charge of the Common Market. On the Carter's flight home to Washington, Rosalynn sat informally on the floor of the plane, her head resting in Jimmy's lap as he answered reporters' questions. It had been one of the most exciting weeks of her life.

*   *   *

A few Rosalynn-watchers have commented that she is at her best when she is playing the proud mother role with Amy. During a four-nation trip that Rosalynn and Amy made with Jimmy in April 1978, the women of Badagry, Nigeria took them both to their hearts.

Both mother and daughter, wearing large Nigerian straw hats, visited the Badagry marketplace, enjoying native sweetmeats and accepting a shopping basket full of flowers. Amy, walking hand in hand with a black child, found the visit a living geography lesson. The entire family attended a Baptist church service and later joined some thirty thousand Nigerians who had come to watch the American President and First Lady be entertained by dancers from the nation's nineteen states. Everybody laughed when Jimmy found it hard going to shake hands with a dancer on stilts.

In Brasilia, Brazil, Amy played soccer. In Rio de Janeiro, Rosalynn was treated to a visit to one of the city's fabled nightclubs. And during a four-hour visit to Liberia, which was founded by former American slaves in 1822, Jimmy, Rosalynn, and Amy lunched with President William R. Tolbert, Jr.

Amy's favorite moments were the fiesta greeting they received in Venezuela and of course the hustle and bustle of a real African marketplace. For Rosalynn the special moments were watching Jimmy lay a wreath at the tomb of Simon Bolívar, the Venezuelan patriot, and deliver an address in Nigeria's National Theatre. His theme was the deliverance of Africans from all racial injustice. His voice cracked with emotion as he said: "And on that day blacks and whites alike will be able to say, in the words of a great man from my own state, Dr. Martin Luther King, Jr., 'Free at last! Free at last! Great God almighty, we are free at last!' "

Jimmy Carter had made history by being the first American president to make a state visit to black Africa. Seven days later, the Carter family was home in Washington. Amy had plenty to tell her friends when she went back to school.

*   *   *

_19_

"ROS, what think?" the President sometimes scribbles on a memo for his wife. He is forever telling his assistants what Rosalynn thinks. Her opinion is obviously very important to him.

"People have written that I'm Jimmy's greatest adviser and so forth. I'm not," says Rosalynn. "But I talk to him about all the things he's trying to do. If there's something that involves the elderly, women's issues, the mentally ill, things that I know about, that I feel I can advise him on, I do it. And he trusts my opinion because he knows that I've worked on these things for a long time. I don't even try to advise him on a lot of things. But I can talk to him about what I feel ought to be done. He talks to me about welfare, tax reform, and I tell him what I think about it. I don't say, do this or do that, I've never done that, And I'm not saying that he always does what I want him to do. But he always listens."

Although, once the Carters took up residence in Washington, detractors began calling Rosalynn the "Iron Lady," just as during the presidential campaign they dubbed her the "Steel Magnolia," Rosalynn turned a deaf ear to their remarks. If she had chosen more popular causes to champion, such as Jacqueline Kennedy's refurbishing of the White House or Lady Bird Johnson's beautification of America project, Rosalynn might have had more notice in the national press. Mental health programs, important as they were, just did not capture the public imagination in the same way.

*   *   *

Following her return from the successful Latin America tour, the First Lady devoted her time to her first major public project, the President's Commission on Mental Health. Jimmy gave her full credit for this, one of the first Executive Orders he signed after taking office.

Upon entering the Executive Mansion, Rosalynn had promised that mental health programs and care of the elderly would be her first concerns. "Rosalynn is responsible for many of the improvements we made in Georgia's mental-health program," said Jimmy. "Because she persuaded me of the urgency of this problem, I want to attack it on a national scale. She is an expert in the field, and she'll be as effective nationally as she was in Georgia."

Having persuaded the President to appoint a twenty-member commission, Rosalynn agreed to serve as honorary chairman. As the President's wife, she cannot legally serve as the official chairman, but this did not prevent Rosalynn from working tirelessly for the commission. During that first spring of Jimmy Carter's administration, she chaired mental health meetings across the nation. In May she held the first in a series of round-table discussions at the White House on the problems of the aging.

Rosalynn worked for some three hundred hours at meetings dealing with the care of mental patients. The emphasis was on shifting patients from large state hospitals into smaller, more homey community centers. Day after day

163

Rosalynn is thanked by Vancouver, B.C., Mayor Jack Volrich after her speech there to a meeting of mental health experts. *Wide World Photos*

she personally studied 117 long range recommendations that would make mental health a national priority.

She was also instrumental in getting the President, against the opposition of the all important Office of Management and Budget, to authorize $300 million for community mental health programs. When the press paid little attention to her efforts she shrugged it off with the observation, "I haven't worked on an image. My purpose is not so much to be visible as to do a good job."

During discussions of the 1979 Federal Budget, Jimmy at first approved a proposal for a general hold-down policy toward mental health programs, for which the appropriations had been doubled in the last budget. Rosalynn argued that an exception should be made for mental health. The debate became heated, but Rosalynn firmly held her ground. The officials finally agreed with her point of view, and Jimmy later reversed his decision to the point of recommending mental health increases amounting to some $42 million.

"We are close, and I do question the things he does," Rosalynn explained. "It's important to question him, argue with him, about whether this is the right thing to do or not. I can agree with him when I agree and disagree when I disagree without hesitation, and that's good."

*   *   *

During the 1978 visit to New Delhi, India, she was asked about press reports "that you speak softly but you carry a big stick."

"Maybe I do speak softly," she answered with a smile, "and maybe I do have some influence with my husband. Maybe that is the big stick."

On the same occasion, she was asked if she thought it "unimaginable" that a woman might succeed to the White

165

House as President. "I don't think it unimaginable. I think it is just a matter of time," she replied.

At another time, when she was asked if she thought she should be paid for all the work she does for the country, Rosalynn simply replied, "Jimmy's salary is sufficient."

*   *   *

At Chicago's North-western Hospital's Institute of Psychiatry, Rosalynn visited with young mothers who had been under treatment for drug addiction. Feeding a baby boy named Michael, she talked with his happy mother, identified only as Darlene, asking her if she were glad that she had given up hard drugs. Michael's mama looked at her son and smilingly admitted, "This was hard, but I'm sure glad that I stuck with it. Isn't he wonderful. That's why I'm glad I stuck with it." There were about seventy women in the program, of which about a dozen were pregnant.

In April 1977 during a brief visit to Plains, Jimmy chatted with a troop of mentally retarded Boy Scouts who were planning to take part in the Special Olympics for the Handicapped to be held in Dalton, Georgia. The President was happy to tell them, "My wife is very interested in the Special Olympics. It's a good program. . . . The nice thing about it is that everybody wins."

*   *   *

In December 1977, Rosalynn achieved star status in the eyes of all the children attending Public School 180 in New York's Harlem. She was there to open a new Cities-to-School program. Clutching the enormous bouquet of chrysanthemums presented to her by Ursula Bruggs, eleven, the First Lady said, "Jimmy and I talk a lot about how to solve the problems confronting us. I believe the answer is in the community. . . . The children are so important. We must bring the services to them, we must let them know we care. I think that's what the program is all about."

Then, as she entered the school lunchroom, a chorus sang out in boisterous welcome, "Consider Yourself at Home."

Later she drove down to Greenwich Village to visit elderly residents of the Village Nursing Home on Hudson Street. There she was greeted by Marian Tanner, seventy-seven, who found instant fame several years ago when her nephew, the late Patrick Dennis, made her the model for his famous book *Auntie Mame*. She was seated next to the First Lady for the turkey lunch. Luigi Vassalo, ninety-three, gave Rosalynn a large button that read, "I helped save the Village Nursing Home."

The Caring Community, a coalition of community groups, raised $100,000 to keep the home open and its purchase option alive. Many of the home's residents have lived in the area all their lives.

_20_

"TIME is running out. We must get the ERA ratified," said Rosalynn Carter speaking at an ERA ball in Tampa, Florida. "I'm willing to help in whatever way I can."

In spite of opponents to the Equal Rights Amendment, the controversial women's equality measure, who called the visit "an unethical use of public funds," Rosalynn made her point. She also insisted that the government paid for only the first part of her trip, which took her to Orlando where she dedicated a $30,000 fountain placed in front of the United States Court House.

Later on September 18, 1978, Rosalynn speaking at a White House meeting called by Sarah Weddington, adviser to President Carter on women's issues, asked some fifty female presidential appointees to "assume a leadership role and just work" for an extension of the deadline to ratify the Equal Rights Amendment.

Rosalynn maintained that both the President and she were personally involved in the extension fight. At that time, the House had approved a measure to extend the ratification deadline to June 30, 1982, but the Senate had yet to act.

In addition to the First Lady's interest in ERA, Second Lady Joan Mondale was equally involved in the issue. Addressing the wives of thirty Senators in her home she said that the extension prospects "look very grim" but "we expect to change that."

ERA had been ratified by 35 of the 38 states required by law, but without the extension it was given no chance of surviving. Feminist Betty Friedan bluntly told the gathering that if the extension were not passed in the following two weeks "our daughters' daughters will have to start all over again."

The legislation giving a time extension for the ratification of ERA finally passed, and President Carter signed it into law on October 20, 1978.

*　　*　　*

At the 1977 National Women's Conference in Houston, Texas, Rosalynn was joined by former First Ladies Lady Bird Johnson and Betty Ford. In her speech Rosalynn begged those present to avoid "the defensiveness and anger" that could divide the feminist and conservative delegates from across the nation. Speaking in a clear voice, she said: "There have been a lot of disagreements and conflicts, but I agree with my daughter-in-law, Judy, that we must guard against obscuring valid issues with defensiveness and anger."

Appealing to conservatives who intimated they were against feminism for religious reasons, Rosalynn, whose deep religious convictions were known to those present, had these words of caution: "The glue that holds us together is the firm knowledge that our basic goals are the same. All of us cherish our freedom to live, to worship, to vote, to work as we please."

Rosalynn received an ovation filled with cheers when she restated Jimmy's commitment to equality for women and recited a long list of women in major administration jobs.

*   *   *

Back in the White House Rosalynn resumed her own post in the administration with her usual efficiency. She was forced to find a new way to her office from the family quarters in order to escape the tourists. It was through the basement. Explained her Press Secretary, Mary Hoyt,

"It isn't that the First Lady doesn't like tourists—just that she gets tired of stopping and chatting with them every day. Since tour groups are going through the White House about the time Mrs. Carter is going to and from her office, she had to find another route. . . . So now she goes through the basement."

Both Jimmy and Rosalynn were finding that life in the Executive Mansion was far from private. While he had visibly aged since campaigning days, Rosalynn looked young and fresh as ever.

*   *   *

Rosalynn was delighted when, in October 1978, Jimmy signed a special bill authorizing the U.S. Mint to replace the large Eisenhower dollar with another bearing the likeness of suffragette Susan B. Anthony (1820–1906). This would be the first time that the likeness of an American woman has appeared on an American coin. It was Susan, then nearing thirty, who observed the family of a cousin as the latter gave birth to a child and who shortly afterward wrote home bluntly expressing her opinion that certain drawbacks to marriage made a woman quite content to remain single. Instead of choosing marriage and motherhood, Susan gave all her passions to reform.

*　　*　　*

Rosalynn was glad to have a woman as one of her Secret Service guards. She has always been grateful for the care they give her and Amy, and will never forget the time at a Virginia pet show that the guards saved Amy from being trampled by, of all animals, an elephant. Rosalynn and the guards were more upset than the child, who was quick to forgive the bewildered animal.

*　　*　　*

Many observers of the Carter administration have felt that the seriousness and competence that Rosalynn brings to her role of First Lady has done much to advance the cause of feminism around the world.

Rosalynn was glad to become Honorary Chairwoman of the Friendship Force, created by then Governor Jimmy Carter in 1973 when he travelled to Brazil. Wayne Smith, executive director of the Friendship Force, said: "With participants paying their own way, it is estimated the average price would be $300 to $400 for a ten-day trip, regardless of the nation visited."

Rosalynn also accompanied Jimmy to the special annual dinner at the Gridiron, a newspapermen's club which for years had been strictly for men only. The previous year, because she was a woman, her husband had been invited, but she had not.

Other Southern First Ladies

MARTHA Washington, America's first First Lady, and Rosalynn Carter have something in common—their love of gardening, fresh vegetables, and cooking.

Often known as the "Mother of Our Country," Martha Dandridge Custis Washington (1732–1802) lived at the time of her marriage to George Washington in The White House, located by the York River, Virginia. She never lived in the Washington White House for in her day it had not been built.

She was a 27-year-old widow with two young children when she married George on January 6, 1759. For the ceremony she chose a quilted petticoat of white satin, a corded silk skirt with point lace and ruffles, and white satin slippers adorned with sparkling diamond buckles.

Martha was very much the peacemaker, bringing harmony to her husband's officers at his Cambridge Headquarters during the American Revolution. She simply made friends with their wives.

In March, 1777, she braved freezing winter weather to reach Washington's headquarters in Morristown, New Jersey. There she nursed her own husband back to health, formed a sewing group among the officers wives to make much needed clothing for the troops, and generally cheered everybody. On one occasion, a group of fine Morristown women decided to call upon Martha and were surprised at what they found. A Mrs. Troupe recorded the visit:

"We dressed ourselves in our most elegant ruffles and silks, and were introduced to her ladyship. . . . We found her knitting and with a specked apron on! There we were without a stitch of work and sitting in State, but General Washington's lady was knitting stockings."

When the war was over and Washington became the new nation's first President, Martha wrote: "I had little thought when the war was finished that any circumstance could possibly happen which would call the General into public life again. I had anticipated, from that moment, we should be suffered to grow old together in solitude and tranquility. That was the first and dearest wish of my heart."

Finally, her husband's presidency over, Martha returned with him to their beloved plantation, Mount Vernon, in Virginia. From there she wrote the wife of General Knox, whom she had known during the war: "I cannot tell you how much I enjoy home after being deprived of one so long. . . . I am again fairly settled down to the pleasant duties of an old-fashioned Virginia housekeeper, steady as a clock, busy as a bee, and cheerful as a cricket." She was then 66.

Unfortunately they knew little privacy, for visitors, many they did not even know, descended upon Mount Vernon to pay their respects to the "Old Man," as Washington was affectionately known, and his venerable lady. Because of their many guests Washington felt obliged to provide his wife with a housekeeper. Somewhat testily he confided to his diary, "Would anyone believe that, with 101 cows, I am still obliged to buy butter for my family?"

Two years later on December 14, 1799, he caught cold and died.

As a young plantation mistress, before the exciting days of war followed by the presidency, Martha lived a life that was domestic and full. She had to order the meals, supervise the cooking, and see that the table was set. She saw that "pease" were sown at the proper time; that the herbs were picked and dried; and that enough cloth was spun to make apparel for her family and the many slaves. Once she had sixteen spinning wheels set up in a spinning house complete with all the looms, flaxbrakes, and domestic machinery that went with them. She made medicines and tonics and a special powder to keep teeth clean and white, and, in the case of her husband who had a set of false dentures, "to fasten them."

Martha survived her dear George for three and a half years. She was efficient to the end, even laying out her own funeral dress before she died.

*   *   *

"Two messengers, covered with dust, came to bid me fly, but here I mean to wait for him [her husband, the President]. Our kind friend Mr. Carroll has come to hasten my departure and is in a very bad humor with me because I insist on waiting until the large picture of General Washington is secured, and it requires to be unscrewed from the wall. This process is found too tedious for these perilous moments; I have ordered the frame to be broken and the canvas taken out. It is done, and the precious portrait placed in the hands of two gentlemen of New York for safekeeping."

The writer was Dolly Madison, wife of President James Madison, one of the most popular and flamboyant First La-

174

dies ever to grace the White House. In addition to saving George Washington's portrait from the British Army in 1812, an act that made her a national heroine, Dolly rescued her macaw, one of the first White House pets to be recorded.

Born May 20, 1768, in what is now Guildford County, North Carolina, Dolly was the daughter of John Payne, a Quaker. Her first husband was a Philadelphia lawyer named John Todd. It was Aaron Burr who introduced Dolly to James Madison. Martha Washington gave her blessing to their marriage in 1794.

Madison was twenty years her senior, and she was three inches taller than he. "My darling little husband," Dolly liked to call him.

Dolly's only child, John Payne Todd, was a failure in many ways and a life-long worry to his mother, but he did leave his mark on White House domestic history. He told Dolly that in ancient Egypt the children had rolled gaily decorated eggs against the base of the pyramids. Dolly thought the idea a good one, and since there were no pyramids in Washington, decided to use the Capitol lawns instead.

She personally colored hundreds of hard boiled eggs with dye, inviting the city's children to an egg rolling on Easter Monday, a custom that has survived succeeding administrations and is now traditionally held on the White House lawn.

After her exciting years as First Lady, Dolly dutifully returned home to Montpelier, Virginia, where she personally cared for her sick husband and his 85-year-old mother. The old lady lived to be 97 and James Madison, due it was said to his wife's devoted care, to the age of 85.

She spent her last years in Washington, a sprightly old lady inclined to wear turbans. Congress granted her the franking privilege. She died greatly beloved on July 12,

1849, and was laid to rest in the Congressional Cemetery. It was only fitting that six years later her body was taken back to Montpelier to be buried beside her "darling little husband."

*   *   *

"Daughter, I will put you in the White House if it costs me my life."

So wrote former president Andrew Jackson, popularly known as "Old Hickory," to his "dear Sally," Sarah Childress Polk, whom he always liked to call "Daughter." Sarah had been a dear friend of Jackson's beloved wife, Rachael, whose maligning by his political enemies had hastened her death. Rachael never lived to be First Lady.

It was Andrew Jackson, some historians say, who urged young James Polk to marry Sally Childress, eldest daughter of Captain Joel Childress, a wealthy merchant of Murfreesboro, Tennessee, where she had been born, August 14, 1803. Although it was not considered necessary to send daughters to school like sons, Mrs. Childress paid the headmaster of her only son, Anderson's, school to give private lessons to Sarah and her younger sister, Susan. Later both girls were sent to a girls school in Nashville, where they boarded in the home of Colonel Butler, a staff officer of General Andrew Jackson. That was when Sarah began to call him 'Uncle Andrew.' At 15 years old Sarah was enrolled in the Salem, North Carolina, Female Academy, where her studies were cut short by Captain Childress' death. In 1820 she returned home to live with her mother.

From the time of their marriage, New Year's Day 1824, Sarah's life and ambitions were completely centered around her 'Jim' as she called him, in much the same way that Rosalynn Carter's have been for Jimmy. There are many interesting parallels between the Polks and the present occupants of the White House.

176

James Polk had been so sickly as a boy that he had been unable to attend regular school. His father, Samuel Polk, a farmer, taught him at home. Even so, when James had a gallstone operation at the age of 14, the doctor noted he was 'uncouth and uneducated.'

Samuel decided that, late as it was, his son, who was too frail for farming, must have an education in order to learn a profession. James proved so able a student that he was able to graduate as salutatorian from the University of North Carolina in 1818. At 26 he opened his own law office. It was Sarah who asked James to run for the State Legislature, and with her help, Andrew Jackson approved his candidacy. Because he was only 5 feet 7 inches tall, he was nick-named "Napoleon of the Stump."

Little more than a year after their marriage, James Polk won a seat in the United States House of Representatives. Sarah stayed home for the first year, sending regular reports to her husband of happenings in his district. In 1826 she joined him in Washington, where she amazed many of the other political wives by refusing to attend parties without her husband. "I wouldn't have a good time without Jim, so there's no use going," she said.

When Jackson became President in 1828, James became one of his most trusted spokesmen. They both shared the same interest in States Rights.

James served in Congress for fourteen years, and for two terms as Speaker of the House. Sarah later said that the Speaker could have "even more power and influence over legislation and in directing the policy of parties than the President or any other public officer."

Spurred on by Sarah, James set his sights on the presidency. Jackson thought that his protégé would achieve this better if he first ran for the Governorship of his native Tennessee, which he did and won.

As First Lady of her state Sarah was never separated from her husband. As the new Governor told her, "Why stay home? To take care of the house? If the house burns down, we can live without it."

Governor Polk ran for reelection twice and on both occasions was defeated. When he announced he was a candidate for the presidency of the United States, the Democrats were amazed. "Who is James Polk?" they were asking just as their political descendants demand before the 1976 Presidential campaign—"Jimmy who?"

When the convention delegates could not decide on the merits of General Lewis Cass as opposed to Martin Van Buren, the ailing Jackson stepped in, and James Polk was accepted as a compromise. In the election that followed, Polk was the victor over Henry Clay, the favored Whig candidate.

As Andrew Jackson promised, his dear Sally went to the White House.

There the new First Lady made history of her own as confidential secretary to her husband, the President. She had a desk in his office, read all the newspapers and clipped items that she thought he should see.

At 50, James Polk was the youngest man ever elected to the Presidency. His wife, then 41, was still a strikingly beautiful woman with a pale Spanish skin and jet black hair. It had poured with rain on James's Inauguration Day, and few could hear the speech she had so carefully helped him prepare.

They both hated parties, considering them to be a waste of valuable time. Polk insisted they were "hired to work." After a White House celebration, he would toil late into the night, with Sarah at his side, to make up for the hours they had "lost." They kept a rigidly Spartan household, Sarah keeping a watchful eye on the First Family finances.

Sarah had an extraordinary knowledge of government. The future President Franklin Pierce said that he much preferred talking politics with Mrs. Polk than with anyone else, and that included her husband.

As for the President he loved to publicly praise his wife's wisdom. It was no secret that he relied upon her opinions and advice more than anybody else's. While a New York newspaper dubbed Sarah "the President's guardian angel," Polk confessed "None but Sarah knew so intimately my private affairs." He refused to run for a second term so that, without distraction, he could devote his entire Presidency to the good of the growing nation.

Sarah Polk is credited with bringing gaslight into the White House, but she refused to remove the candlelit chandelier in the reception hall. Once the gas jets mysteriously went out at a party, but the beautiful candlelight remained.

When they eventually left the White House for their own home, "Polk Place" in Nashville, Sarah admitted that it felt "like Christmas." Unfortunately, as President, her husband had completely exhausted his strength by his long working hours. He died a few weeks after moving into their new home. Sarah buried him on the front lawn.

Living for many years as the guardian of his memory she delighted in showing visitors their treasured books and mementoes of the White House years, which she always dusted herself. She still considered herself to be "the property of nation," and during the sad years of the War Between the States, she was respected by both Confederate and Union troops. Polk Place was kept inviolate.

As a very old lady in her widow's weeds (she was nearly 88 when she died in 1891), Sarah Childress Polk would stand by her husband's grave and quietly repeat the last words he had spoken on his deathbed:

"I love you, Sarah, for all eternity, I love you."

*   *   *

Kentucky-born Mary Todd Lincoln was the most tragic and controversial of all the Southern First Ladies. During the War between the States, gossip mongers maliciously dubbed her "The Spy in the White House."

Her family had never thought the struggling young lawyer Abraham Lincoln good enough for one of their own but Mary was a shrewd judge of greatness. In 1847, complimented on her husband's character, she replied, "Yes, he is a great favorite everywhere. He is to be President of the United States some day; if I had not thought so I never would have married him, for you can see he is not pretty. But look at him. Doesn't he look as if he would make a magnificent President."

All her life she suffered from terrible headaches, which grew even worse as she got older. Wrote a concerned Lincoln in 1848, "Are you entirely free from headache? That is good—good considering it is the first spring you have been free from it since we were acquainted. . . . I am afraid you will get so well, and fat, and young, as to be wanting to marry again."

Criticized daily in the press during her White House sojourn, Mary told young Mary Harlan, "You should go out every day and enjoy yourself—trouble comes soon enough, my dear child. . . . I know full well by experience, power and high position do not ensure a bed of roses."

When her small son Willie died, she never went into his bedroom again. She banned flowers from the White House because he had loved them.

During this sad period, President Lincoln befriended a young postal worker, Vinnie Ream, who was allowed to take her tub of clay to the White House to model his head. Vinnie recorded that Lincoln often rose from his desk and walked over to the window, looking down into the gardens as if expecting to see Willie still at play. When he turned to face her again, tears would be streaming down his face.

Lincoln's assassination was a blow from which Mary never recovered. She was too ill to attend his funeral. When she attempted to sell her expensive gowns to help pay off her debts, she was crucified in the newspapers. Bitterly she said, "If I had committed murder in every state in this blessed Union, I could not be more traduced. An ungrateful country this."

Committed to an insane asylum for a time by her eldest son, Robert, Mary knew no peace. The final blow was the death of her younger son, Tad, who had been her constant companion in a self-imposed exile that had even taken them to Europe.

Sick and broken in spirit she spent her last days at Springfield, Illinois, in the home of her sister, Mrs. Ninian Edwards, lying in a darkened room with her memories. On her finger was the wedding band that Abraham had given her upon which were engraved the words, "Love is Eternal."

Mary Todd Lincoln died on July 16, 1882. At last she was reunited with Abraham and at her funeral the minister likened them to two tall trees . . . One of them was suddenly felled by a storm leaving the other exposed to the elements.

*　　*　　*

Rosalynn Carter was not the first Southern First Lady to take her sewing machine to the White House. Edith Bolling Wilson, second wife of President Woodrow Wilson and the daughter of a Virginia judge, also brought hers along. She was 42 years old, the widow of Norman Galt, a Washington jeweler, and had married the President only fifteen months after the death of his first wife, Georgia-born Ellen Louise Axson Wilson. The first Mrs. Wilson had been a talented painter and was responsible for making a rose garden at the White House.

During their controversial courtship, Woodrow and Edith met secretly at 12 West Tenth Street, New York City, an old, red brick mansion, where Emily Post, the famed etiquette authority, and Isabel Lydia Whitney, America's first woman fresco painter, had each spent part of their lives. Secret Service agents lined the front steps and winding inner staircase the day that the President and his future wife ate Thanksgiving dinner there. The aged butler could not find the silver gravy boat for the meal and, to his chagrin, had to use an ordinary oatmeal bowl.

The wedding took place in the bride's home on December 18, 1915. She wore a black velvet gown with long, pointed sleeves and a large, black, beaver picture hat. Her wedding ring was made from a solid gold nugget, the gift from the people of California.

Woodrow whistled "Oh, You Beautiful Doll" on their honeymoon. He also danced a cakewalk and a jig.

During World War I, Edith kept a flock of sheep on the White House lawns, just as the Carters had done on state-owned grass during Jimmy's governorship of Georgia. Edith raised $100,000 for the Red Cross from the wool. She also christened merchant vessels, giving them American Indian names in memory of Princess Pocahontas, whose lineal descendant she was. Her contributions as a Red Cross worker were enormous. She personally answered letters from fathers and mothers whose sons were missing in action.

After President Wilson's collapse following a speech made in Pueblo, Colorado, in September 1919, news of his serious condition was kept from the nation, including the fact that he had actually suffered a stroke and was partially paralyzed. Americans were simply told that their President was ill.

For seventeen months, Edith and Dr. Cary T. Grayson cared for Woodrow. All state papers were submitted to his wife. It was rumored that the doctor and first Lady were running the country. The First Lady was hurt when a newspaper referred to the period as "the Mrs. Wilson Regency." She called it, "My stewardship."

President Wilson lived to complete his White House term, not dying until February 3, 1924. Until her own death in 1962, Edith Bolling Wilson was a popular figure in Washington. For some years she made an annual pilgrimage to Geneva, Switzerland, headquarters of the League of Nations in which her husband had believed so much. In 1931, she unveiled his statue given by Ignace Jan Paderewski, the pianist and statesman, which had been erected in Poland.

She found personal satisfaction in knowing that her husband was the only American President to be buried in Washington's National Cathedral.

*　　*　　*

They called Lady Bird Johnson the "First Lady of Beautification" while she lived in the White House. Lady Bird beautified the streets of Washington—even the poorer districts—with flowering shrubs and trees.

"Ugliness—the gray, dreary, unchanging world of deprived neighborhoods—has contributed to riots, mental ill health, and to crime," said Lady Bird in her simple, direct way, addressing a joint meeting of the American Forestry Association and the National Council of State Garden Clubs in Grand Teton National Park, Wyoming.

Predicting the passing of the highway beautification bill that later became law, she added, "Even though we do not get all the features we want, if we get a measure of them, it will be a step forward."

Lady Bird was a Christmas baby. She was born on a crisp, wintry morning in Karnack, Texas, December 22,

1912. Her black nurse called her "purty as a Lady Bird." Lady Bird's father was Thomas Jefferson Taylor II, familiarly known to the neighbors as "Cap." Outside his general store was the sign:

T. J. TAYLOR
DEALER IN EVERYTHING

He was a clever businessman, who over the years acquired two cotton gins and much land. He had married Minnie Lee Pattillo of Billingsley, Alabama, a cultured and studious woman, whose bookshelves would have pleased a college professor. By the time Lady Bird was five, her mother had introduced her to the mysteries of Roman, Greek, and German mythology. Lady Bird says that the legendary Siegfried with his magic cloak and sword was her own first love.

Minnie Lee did not mix much with the neighbors, but her servants adored her. While Cap Taylor took care of the store and brought in the dollars, his wife played grand opera on the phonograph.

Then, expecting another child, Minnie Lee was ascending the circular staircase when their family pet, a collie dog rushed between her feet, causing her to lose her balance. A miscarriage and blood poisoning followed. Minnie Lee Taylor was only 44 years old when she died on September 14, 1918, leaving a husband and three children including 5-year-old Lady Bird.

Afraid that his adored child might be lonely, Cap Taylor took her to his store every day. He put her cot on the second floor among the row of coffins that he kept as part of his regular stock. Finally, he sent for Minnie Lee's delightful Aunt Effie to come from Alabama and look after Lady Bird.

Aunt Effie, who had never married, was just as unworldly as her late sister. She loved to play the piano as much as Minnie Lee had the phonograph. She encouraged Lady Bird to read books, and by the time the child was eight, she had even read *Ben Hur*.

Aunt Effie liked to invent fantasy friends as they walked through the fields and woods picking wild flowers. "She," Lady Bird recalls of Aunt Effie, "opened my spirit to beauty, but she neglected to give me any insight into the practical matters a girl should know about, such as how to dress or choose one's friends or learn to dance. . . . She was undoubtedly the most unworldly human in the world. She was delicate and airy and very gentle, and she gave me many fine values, which I wouldn't trade for the world."

Every summer they visited relatives in Alabama, where Lady Bird's memories are similar to those of Rosalynn Carter's in Plains. Says Lady Bird, "I remember—who could ever forget?—The laughing hayrides and watermelon suppers, learning to swim in Mulberry Creek, the lazy curl of a cousin's fishing line flickering in the sun, church on Sunday, and then the long Sunday dinner with kinfolks—endless kinsfolk—discussing the endless family gossip around the table."

It was August 1934, in the State Capitol office in Austin, Texas, of her close friend, Eugenia (Gene) Boehringer, that Lady Bird met Lyndon Baines Johnson for the first time. She thought him "excessively thin" and the most outspoken man she had ever met. "I knew I had met something remarkable, but I didn't quite know what."

When she finally took Lyndon home, Cap Taylor bluntly said, "Daughter, you've brought a lot of boys home. This time you've brought a man."

Cap asked Lyndon to stay the night, and, as the pump wasn't working, one of the servants fetched his bath water in pails from the reservoir. That night he proposed to Lady

Bird. When she told her father, he sagely replied, "Some of the best bargains are made in a hurry."

Seven weeks later Lyndon and Lady Bird were married in San Antonio's historic St. Mark's Episcopal Church. Lyndon sent a friend over to Sear's Roebuck to buy the wedding ring, which cost $2.98. Said Lady Bird, "He crowded enough into that courtship to last us all our days. . . ."

The newlyweds settled in Washington where Lyndon earned $267 a month as a congressman's secretary. The magic combination that would lead Lyndon and Lady Bird to the White House had begun.

In 1963, the tragic assassination of President John F. Kennedy swept Lyndon into office, and in 1964, Lady Bird was actively campaigning to elect him in his own right. The Republican candidate was Senator Barry Goldwater.

Lady Bird was given—or rather gave herself—some of the toughest campaign territory to cover by herself—her native South. Because of the controversial Civil Rights Bill, it was then solidly conservative and Goldwater territory. Travelling from city to city on her campaign train, *The Lady Bird Special*, she could not have found it an easy trip, for at times young hecklers, some not old enough even to vote, assailed her with verbal harassment that was often revolting.

When she first set out on October 7, wearing a favorite bright red suit, Lyndon saw her off with the words, "She is one of the greatest campaigners in America. . . . I'm proud that I'm her husband." Lyndon was elected President by a landslide victory, and Lady Bird held the Johnson family Bible at his Inauguration.

Like Eleanor Roosevelt, Lady Bird was always on good terms and accessible to the press. Liz Carpenter became the first working newspaperwoman to hold the job of press secretary to a First Lady. The President had told her, "Go and help Lady Bird." She did just that.

"My job," noted Liz, "is to help Mrs. Johnson help the President. I have known Mrs. Johnson for twenty years, and I can tell you emphatically she is not trying to establish a new identity or a new image or a new sphere of influence or a new anything. She is simply trying to be the best wife she knows how to a husband whose job is President of the United States."

A visit to the White House during the Johnson's Presidency was pure delight. It was as if they had given it back to the American people. And Liz Carpenter offered the visiting writer coffee and cookies. If they had a sweet tooth, there would even be chocolate candies.

Thanks to Lady Bird's determination, a portrait of Eleanor Roosevelt was at last hung in the White House entrance hall, "where," said Lady Bird, "as many people as possible may see it." On January 31, 1966, Mrs. Johnson unveiled the portrait by Douglas Chandor and spoke with admiration of the woman who had lived in the White House for twelve years—longer than any other First Lady: "When I first looked at Douglas Chandor's portrait of Eleanor Roosevelt, I was struck by the artist's use of Mrs. Roosevelt's hands. They are many hands, busy with all kinds of things, and nothing could be more appropriate. For Eleanor Roosevelt was a woman who had hands for the whole world—fine, strong, sensitive hands that enobled everything they touched."

Of all the First Ladies it is Eleanor Roosevelt that Rosalynn Carter has most tried to follow with her work for suffering humanity.

Even though Lyndon isn't with her any more, Lady Bird Johnson leads a full and useful life in her widowhood. Fortunate are those among the hundreds of tourists who meet her while visiting the Johnson ranch country in Texas. Proudly, she shows them her husband's grave in the family cemetery on the banks of the Pedernales River.

Not long ago she was spearheading another conservation project—this time wild flowers. Millions of seeds were scattered on the grass verges along the Texas highways. She sat proudly and listened as President Gerald R. Ford spoke at the official opening of the national memorial to her beloved Lyndon, the Lyndon Baines Johnson Memorial Grove in Washington, D.C. The park is made up of a grove of pines, dogwood trees, clumps of yellow daffodils and walking trails. Lyndon's name is inscribed on a hugh rock of natural granite.

Lady Bird was back in Washington to attend the funeral of Senator Hubert Humphrey, Vice-President during Lyndon's Administration. She was escorted down the Capitol steps behind President and Mrs. Carter by Vice-President and Mrs. Mondale, who each held one of her arms.

The moments she remembers best says Lady Bird Johnson are "the golden moments I had spent in some lovely spot, working in my garden where I added three trees to make a quadrangle with an apple tree."

For her own epitaph she would like the words,

SHE PLANTED THREE TREES

Epilogue

ROSALYNN Carter has proved herself to have the strength of a Scarlett O'Hara coupled with the loving loyalty of a Melanie Wilkes. She comes from that same breed of Southern women who in our own generation has produced such outstanding examples as Coretta Scott King, Lady Bird Johnson, and her own mother-in-law, Lillian Gordy Carter.

Prior to the Camp David Summit when Rosalynn's husband acted as mediator for the President of Egypt and the Prime Minister of Israel, his popularity had dropped to a new low. It was then that a leading newspaper suggested that the President send "Rosalynn to the Rescue." During the presidential election campaign, she had played a leading role.

People in the crowd identify with Rosalynn Carter. She was not born with a silver spoon in her mouth. All her life she has worked for her living. As a wife, daughter, mother, and grandmother, the youthful, pretty Mrs. Carter comes through with flying colors. It was only natural, then, that she take an important role interpreting her husband's policies and presenting them to the public.

Rosalynn and Jimmy Carter stand with Chinese Vice Premier Teng Hsiao-Ping and his wife at the White House as they say good-bye. *Wide World Photos*

The First Lady led the United States delegation at the funeral of Pope Paul VI in Rome, a role that her mother-in-law would repeat at the ceremonies for Pope John Paul I, who died after a reign of only thirty-four days. Of Pope John Paul, Rosalynn was quick to praise "his warmth, his openness, and his love."

She stuck up for the American way of life in her outspoken rebuttal of Alexander Solzhenitzsyn, the exiled Russian novelist whose criticisms of American movies and preoccupations had made headline news throughout the country. This rebuttal was made at the National Press Club in Washington, where Mrs. Carter had the honor of being the first President's wife invited to speak since Eleanor Roosevelt.

Like an all-American wife, she accompanied her husband and daughter in a rubber launch down Idaho's Salmon River, rode horseback beside him in Wyoming's Grand Teton National Park, and ate the fish that he caught for supper.

While the all-important summit talks were going on at Camp David, Rosalynn stood out like a welcome light encouraging, praising, sympathizing with her husband in his monumental—and as it turned out—successful task of getting Begin and Sadat into a conciliatory mood of negotiation over such obstacles as the fate of Israel's West Bank.

Rosalynn is credited with getting the talks off on the right foot. Seeking for a common thread among the three leaders—Begin, Sadat, and her own husband—she came to the conclusion that it lay in their individual deep religious convictions. Then she approached Jimmy with the suggestion that they begin their conference with a joint statement made by the three leaders in which they asked for the prayers of the peoples of the world in their search for a lasting Middle-East peace.

Rosalynn listens in the White House Chamber as Israeli Prime Minister Menachem Begin has a whispered word with Egyptian President Anwar Sadat prior to the President's address before a joint session of Congress. *Wide World Photos*

As President Carter addressed Congress on the success of the summit, she sat between President Sadat and Prime Minister Begin, basking in the great ovation accorded her husband.

She had come a long way, this school bus driver's daughter, Plains housewife, and peanut farmer's wife. Rosalynn Smith Carter, the American dream come true. With pride in her heart, she speaks of the future:

"I hope in the coming months—and years—to excite and challenge young and old people in communities across this country to become a part of what I think is a national movement toward a more caring society, one in which we feel responsible for our neighbor."

Selected
Bibliography

Agee, James. *Collected Short Prose of James Agee*. Houghton, Mifflin Company, Boston, 1968. (Edited with a memoir by Robert Fitzgerald)

Agee, James and Evans, Walker. *Let Us Now Praise Famous Men*. Houghton, Mifflin Company, Boston, 1941.

Boddie, John Bennett, *Seventeenth Century Isle of Wight County, Virginia*; A History of the County. Including Abstracts of the County Records, Chicago Law Printing Company, Chicago, 1938.

Carter, Jimmy. *Why Not the Best? Autobiography*. Nashville, Tenn. Broadman Press, 1975.

Hall, Gordon Langley. *The History of American Evangelism*. Macrae Smith Company, Philadelphia.

Irwin, Grace, *Servant of Slaves*. William B. Eerdmans Publishing Company, Grand Rapids, 1961. (A Biographical novel about John Newton.)

Kucharsky, David. *The Man From Plains*, N. Y. , Harper & Row, 1976.

Moncrieff, A. R. Hope. *Isle of Wight*, Adam and Charles Black, London, 1908. (Includes painting by A. Heaton Cooper.)

Norton, Howard and Slosser, Bob, *The Miracle of Jimmy Carter*, Logos International, Plainfield, N.J. 1976.

Stanford, Phil, Carter: *The Citizen's Guide to the 1976 Presidential Candidates*, Washington, D.C.: Capital Hill News Service, 1976.

Stapleton, Ruth Carter. *The Gift of Inner Healing*. Waco, Texas, Word, 1977.

Wheeler, Leslie, *Jimmy Who?* Woodbury, N. Y. Barron's Educational Series, 1976.